Indian Regional Classics

INDIAN REGIONAL CLASSICS

Fast, Fresh, and Healthy Home Cooking

Julie Sahni

TEN SPEED PRESS
Berkeley • Toronto

A Kirsty Melville Book

Ten Speed Press
P.O. Box 7123
Berkeley, California 94707

Distributed in Australia by Simon and Schuster Australia, Canada by Ten Speed Press Canada,
in New Zealand by Southern Publishers Group, in South Africa by Real Books, in Southeast
Asia by Berkeley Books, and in the United Kingdom and Europe by Airlift Book Company.

Jacket design by Nancy Austin
Text design by Toni Tajima

Library of Congress Cataloging-in-Publication Data
Sahni, Julie.
    Indian regional classics / Julie Sahni.
        p. cm.
    Includes index.
    ISBN 1-58008-345-5
      1. Cookery, India. I. Title

    TX724.5 .S2412   2001
    641.5954—dc21   2001053062

First printing, 2001
Printed in the United States of America

2   3   4   5   6   7   8   9   10   —   05   04   03   02

DEDICATED TO

my beloved father
Dr. Venkataraman Ranganathan Iyer

"STRIVE FOR EXCELLENCE."

CONTENTS

ACKNOWLEDGMENTS

"WRITE a book of simple, delicious food you serve us (family and friends) that will introduce Indian cooking to a novice in a small town, such as Flint, Michigan," said my beloved friend, the late Pierre Franey. He sowed the seeds for this book, for which I am eternally indebted.

I also thank my mother, Padmavati Ranganathan, for helping me gather recipes, and passing along innovative suggestions, saying thing like, "Try Rice Krispies in the fritter batter for a great crunchy texture."

As the book concept became a reality, many colleagues extended generous help and valuable suggestions. In particular Susan Derecskey, who copyedited this book; Pat Adrian of Book of the Month Club for bringing Kirsty Melville, the publisher of Ten Speed Press and me together; Nach Waxman of Kitchen Arts and Letters; Bill Wallace of Draeger's Market; and Daniel Halpern of the Ecco Press.

At Ten Speed Press, I thank my editors, Mariah Bear and Holly Taines White. I am also thankful to Joan Nielsen for her painstakingly meticulous proofreading, and to Nancy Austin and Toni Tajima for an incredibly captivating book design.

INTRODUCTION

WELCOME to the fascinating world of Indian cuisine! Based on the very principles so much in favor today—the preference for healthful wholesome foods and the passion for exciting new flavors—Indian cooking is perfectly suited to the Western kitchen and palate.

I would like to dispel the notion that Indian cooking is exotic, complex, and time consuming. One reason for this misconception is the long list of ingredients, primarily spices, in Indian recipes. But they are there for a reason. While other cuisines use ingredients such as cornstarch, cream, and vinegar to thicken, enrich, and lend a sour taste, Indian cooking uses spices to do all these jobs, plus more. Spices have many properties besides the aromatic and medicinal. Indian cooks have capitalized on all the attributes of spices, and they are the underpinnings of Indian cooking. Mention spices and instantly visions of snake charmers, gaily festooned elephants, and the Taj Mahal shimmering in the moonlight come to mind. Yet it may come as a surprise to find that only a handful of spices are native to India, black pepper, cardamom, turmeric, and kari leaf among them. Most of the spices in curry powder, the famous spice blend from India, are of Mediterranean origin. Cumin, coriander, fennel, mustard, and fenugreek are all native to the Mediterranean Basin. And chiles, too, are an import, introduced by the Portuguese in the early sixteenth century from the New World.

Indian cooking is not one single style of cooking. Rather, it is an amalgamation of several cuisines representing the different geographical features of the nation, its cultural heritage, and the religious beliefs of its people. The terrain and climate of India are indeed extremely varied. They range from snow-covered Kashmir in the northern Himalayan mountains to the sultry Malabar coast in the deep south, from the lush slopes of Darjeeling in the east to the sprawling Rajasthan desert of the west. India has also been gastronomically influenced by invading cultures over the centuries. These include everyone from the Greeks, Arabs, and Mongols to the Portuguese and British.

These shifts in climate, culture, and religious practices have spawned a bountiful array of foods from each region. From the north come mellow yogurt-and-herb marinated and grilled meats, the most famous being tandoori chicken; subtle curries of lamb and kid; smoky pan-roasted vegetables; garlicky lentils; and sweet, fruity yogurt drinks. Braised meat is scented with cumin, fennel, and cardamom and the spice blend called *garam masala.* Bread is the staple there, made with whole-grain flours from wheat, millet, and corn. North India is also the land of fragrant basmati rice. Food is cooked in amber-colored oils pressed from mustard seeds or peanuts and is garnished with fresh coriander and mint.

In the south, the homeland of the Hindu Brahmin and Jain vegetarians, food is more earthy and fiery. Curried stews with lentils, steamed vegetables dressed with coconut and mustard seeds, and assertive tamarind-flavored sauces are common. Rice is the primary grain; in addition to being served plain with each meal, it is made into pancakes, dumplings, and fritters. Coconut milk is used instead of cow's milk, coconut cream instead of yogurt. Food is cooked in aromatic spice-infused oils and flavored with curry powder, shallots, and kari leaves.

To the east lie the fertile plains and shores of Bengal, where fish and seafood, mustard in all its forms, squash, and red lentils rule. Stews and stir-fried vegetables are laced with the garlic and *panch phoron,* a blend of five spices, and tempered with cinnamon and coconut. Fresh coriander, basil, and kari leaves add herbal fragrances.

In the dry regions of western India grow fiber-rich beans and peas, which are cooked with such aromatic spices as ajowan, fennel, and nigella and chiles. Dill and parsley are used as green vegetables. Breads, which are a staple here, are flavored with spices and vegetable purées.

Hindus are the predominant religious group in India. The Jains, Sikhs, and Buddhists, who were all once a part of the Hindu religion, are today distinctly separate communities and form a sizable minority. Together they have laid the foundation of Indian cooking. Their cuisines in their infinite interpretations have come to be known as the regional cooking of India. Of particular importance are two sub-groups: the Hindu Brahmins (one of the four castes of the Hindus) and the Jains. Both are strictly vegetarian, excluding all forms of meat, fish, and their by-products from their diet. Working within their religious taboos and dietary restrictions, these communities have developed a vegetarian cuisine of unparalleled finesse.

Also worth mentioning are those special cultural groups that emerged from foreign influence and whose culinary impact has been profound. Such dishes as the vindaloo of Goa from the Christians of Portuguese descent, shrimp *patia* of Bombay from the Parsis of Persian origin, and kedgeree and foods from the Anglo-Indians are known all over India.

The Muslims are the largest minority group in India. They are credited with introducing the sophisticated Moghul culture to India that gave the world, among other splendors, the Taj Mahal. It was in the royal courts and kitchens of the Moghuls that the most refined of all Indian regional cuisines was born. This style of cooking, with its traces of Persian and Turkish influence, is typified by creamy mellow sauces, subtle fragrances, and exquisite garnishes.

An uncommon array of food exists in India today, ranging from the smoky clay-oven roasted tandoori chicken and *biriyani* pilafs of the Moghuls to the piquant fish curry of the Madras Tamils, from the spice-infused lobster of the Bengalis to the plum-glazed roast duck of the Anglo-Indians. Such dishes represent Indian food in all its intricacies and complexity.

One of the most wonderful aspects of Indian cooking is that complex flavorings are achieved by straightforward cooking techniques. No unfamiliar gadgets need be brought out and mastered. The tools and equipment found in an average Western kitchen, including the food processor and nonstick pans, are more than adequate to perform most of the tasks required in Indian cooking. In other words, Indian cooking is quick and easy, healthy and frugal. All you need to bring to it is a desire to awaken your senses with aromas and flavors.

SPICES AND HERBS IN INDIAN COOKING

INDIAN cooking is the most complexly flavored and the most aromatic of the world's cuisines. This magical property is created by spices and herbs, which are the foundation of Indian cooking. They are used not just to flavor food but to give color, piquancy, heat, and texture to the finished dish. Knowledge of spices and herbs—how they interact with food to bring out the desired flavor—has to be mastered in order to become a natural Indian cook.

In addition to their culinary facet, spices and herbs have medicinal attributes; they are good for the body, mind, and soul. They also act as preservatives, an added benefit since dishes can be prepared ahead and refrigerated for several days without any change in flavor or appearance.

Spices must be cooked in order for them to be digested easily. For this reason, spices are always put into a dish at the start of, or at least early in the cooking. When spices are sprinkled over a finished dish such as a yogurt salad or a drink, they must be precooked. This is done by placing the whole spices in a frying pan and toasting them until they turn several shades darker and give off a roasted aroma. Then they are ground.

Spices should be purchased whole (except for ground ginger, cayenne, and turmeric, which are sold in powdered form only) and stored in airtight containers in a cool, dry place. Spices release more fragrance when crushed, so they are generally added to dishes in ground form. To grind spices, use a spice mill or coffee grinder reserved for grinding spices or a mortar and pestle. Grind only small quantities of spices as needed, as ground spices quickly go stale.

In India, herbs are cultivated all year round and are readily available for use. Both fresh and dried herbs are used in Indian cooking. Fresh herbs—the leaves and tender stems—are chopped and mixed into dishes or used as a garnish. They may also be chopped and mixed with fresh ginger, spices, and yogurt to serve as relishes and dips, or brewed with fresh ginger and honey in herbal teas. The tradition of using dried herbs began in the mountain regions of northern India where extreme weather conditions prevent year-round herb gardening.

Most spices and herbs used in Indian cooking are widely available. A few of the more unusual, such as ajowan (carum or *ajwain*) or nigella (*kalonji*) can be found in Indian or Pakistani grocery shops or through mail order, but in all cases I have given more readily available alternatives.

Finally, remember that spices and herbs are like perfume: They must be handled with a delicate touch—just enough to tease the palate, leaving behind a trail of exotic intrigue and haunting scents.

Spices and Spice Blends

Indian cooks have a way with spices, or masalas. In addition to being added separately during the cooking process, spices are often premixed into blends to produce special flavorings; these are also called masalas. They are an intrinsic part of Indian cooking, lending that special aroma generally associated with a particular dish. *Garam Masala* is the aroma of tandoori chicken, while smoky toasted cumin is that of yogurt salad, for example. The most frequently used prepared spices in the Indian kitchen are three spice blends—Curry Powder, *Garam Masala*, and *Panch Phoron*. All can be made ahead and stored in a cool, dry place.

Curry Powder

The primary flavor in curry powder is coriander with undertones of fenugreek and turmeric. In the past, the mix contained kari leaf, a fragrant balmy herb, but today it contains only spices. This recipe, one of my favorites, contains fennel, which is used by some communities in South India. It has very little red pepper because I do not like my food fiery-hot. I like to enjoy and appreciate the aromatic aspects of the spices as well as the food. If you want it hot and spicy, add more ground red pepper to your taste.

MAKES ABOUT $^1/_2$ CUP

3 tablespoons coriander seeds

2 teaspoons cumin seeds

1 teaspoon fenugreek seeds

1 teaspoon fennel seeds

1 teaspoon yellow mustard seeds

1 to 2 teaspoons white peppercorns

6 whole cloves

2 tablespoons turmeric

1 to 2 teaspoons ground red pepper

1. Put the coriander, cumin, fenugreek, fennel, mustard seeds, peppercorns, and cloves in a dry heavy skillet over medium heat. Toast the spices, stirring occasionally, until they turn dark brown, about 12 minutes. Do not raise the heat to quicken the process, or the spices will brown prematurely, leaving the insides undercooked. Cool completely.

2. Working in batches if necessary, transfer the mixture to a spice mill or coffee grinder and grind to a powder. Mix in the turmeric and red pepper. Use immediately or store in an airtight container in a cool, dry place. (*Curry Powder keeps for 3 months.*)

Garam Masala

This is the most aromatic and fragrant of all Indian spice blends. Used throughout North India in all types of dishes—from appetizers and soups to yogurt salad and main courses—this blend is indispensable to Moghul and North Indian cooking. It is widely available, but my homemade version is more fragrant and, of course, fresher.

MAKES ABOUT $^1/_2$ CUP

2 tablespoons cumin seeds

2 tablespoons coriander seeds

2 tablespoons cardamom seeds

2 tablespoons black peppercorns

1 (3-inch) stick cinnamon, broken up

1 teaspoon whole cloves

1 teaspoon grated nutmeg

$^1/_2$ teaspoon saffron (optional)

(continued)

1. Put the cumin, coriander, cardamom, peppercorns, cinnamon, and cloves in a dry heavy skillet over medium-high heat. Toast the spices, stirring occasionally, until they turn several shades darker and give off a sweet smoky aroma, about 10 minutes. Do not raise the heat to quicken the process, or the spices will brown prematurely, leaving the insides undercooked. Cool completely.

2. Working in batches if necessary, transfer the mixture to a spice mill or coffee grinder and grind to a powder. Stir in the nutmeg and saffron. Use immediately or store in an airtight container in a cool, dry place. (*Garam Masala keeps for 3 months.*)

Panch Phoron

A blend of five whole spices—cumin, fennel, mustard, fenugreek, and nigella—Panch Phoron is a Bengal classic. It is used to flavor fish, vegetables, chutneys, and, on occasion, legumes. Although the blend can be assembled at the last minute since there is no roasting involved, I suggest making it ahead if only because measuring spices takes time.

MAKES ¹/₂ CUP

2 tablespoons cumin seeds

2 tablespoons fennel seeds

2 tablespoons black mustard seeds

1 tablespoon fenugreek seeds

1 tablespoon nigella seeds

Combine all the spices in a jar, cover, and store in a cool, dry place.

Treating a Chile-Scorched Mouth

If when eating a highly spiced dish you feel a need to extinguish the fire, reach first for the chilled sweet yogurt drink called *lassi* (page 172). Recent scientific research shows that the lactic acid present in yogurt works best to counter the burn (experienced as pain) in the mouth and throat caused by the chiles. Starchy foods, such as rice or bread, will also work to some extent. Take one or two swallows followed by a sip of ice water. All these are more efficient than a quaff of beer or wine!

THE INDIAN WAY
OF DINING

THE traditional Indian style of eating, *thali,* is somewhat different from what is customary in the West. Each of the courses is spooned into small individual bowls, which are then neatly arranged on a large (15-inch diameter) rimmed plate or tray. Rice, bread, pickles, and relishes are placed on the plate and this fully arranged *thali* is served to each person. The advantage of this style of serving is that once everyone sits down to eat, the meal proceeds without interruption.

It is not necessary, of course, to conform to the *thali* style of eating in order to enjoy an Indian meal. The Western style of serving separate courses is, in fact, very suitable, and I find it avoids the waste often associated with individual servings where it is hard to judge everyone's preferences and capacity.

To compose a simple meal, serve a main dish consisting of meat, poultry, fish, or vegetables and accompany it with bread or rice. For a more elaborate meal, include a selection of side dishes, such as vegetables, *dals,* and salads. Relishes and chutneys are not essential, but they add texture, herbal scent, and bite to the meal.

Finally, there is no reason why these dishes could not be combined with your everyday Western meal. For example, serve the Chicken Curry (page 104) simply with a nice loaf of bread or pita and a green salad, or serve Cauliflower with Nigella in Ginger Oil (page 135) with fried fish. To get you started and make menu planning easier, I have given serving suggestions with each recipe.

Traditional-Style Eating with Fingers

Most Indians eat with their fingers, which adds a highly sensual accent to the dining experience. Using fingers rather than a fork is also logical, especially when bread is served as an accompaniment. Indian breads, like Mexican flour tortillas or Chinese pancakes, are soft and pliable. It is easy to tear a piece and use it to scoop up or wrap around the food.

SAMPLE MENUS

Papaya and Potato Salad

Steamed Fish in Herb Sauce

Cumin Potatoes

Lemon Pilaf

Quick Saffron Pudding

Lentil Wafers

Goan Warm Mussel Salad

Peach Chutney with
Walnuts and Saffron

Chicken Biriyani

Ginger Limeade

Spinach Fritters

Lamb Curry

Cauliflower with Nigella
in Ginger Oil

Green Pea Pilaf

Indian Rice Pudding with
Cardamom

Mulligatawny

Pan-Grilled Scallops with Ajowan

Curry-Scented Mushrooms

Semolina Pilaf

Mango Fool

The Indian Way of Dining

Shrimp Madras

Tandoori Chicken

Broccoli and Carrots in Garlic-Turmeric Oil

Cool Yogurt and Cucumber Salad

Baked Tandoori Bread

Mango Ice Cream

New Delhi Vegetarian Vegetable Soup

Braised Chickpeas with Spicy Sauce

Roasted Pepper and Mint Yogurt Salad

Peach and Walnut Basmati Pilaf

Savory Yogurt Drink with Mint

Royal Cornish Hen Biriyani with Raisins and Almonds

Hyderabad Chiles Braised in Tamarind Sauce

Sweet Mango Lassi

Bangalore Peanut Soup

Roast Duck with Cinnamon-Plum Glaze

Curried Eggplant with Chutney

Sweet Pumpkin Bread

Spiced Tea

Iced Yogurt Soup with Mint

Spice-Rubbed Grilled Lamb

Green Beans in Fenugreek Oil

Deep-Fried Puffy Bread

Sweet Mango Lassi

Fennel, Tomato, and White Bean Stew with Lucknow Fennel Seeds

Cumin Potatoes

Garlic-Tomato Chutney

Lemon Pilaf

APPETIZERS AND SOUPS

INDIAN appetizers are delicately flavored morsels with intriguing aromas and complex flavors. They might be spiced nuts, crisp fried wafers, spicy fritters, or a cool salad flavored with smoky roasted cumin. You can also serve stuffed breads or savory pastries or small portions of several main courses, including tandoori meats and vegetables, as appetizers.

Although India does not have a tradition of serving soup as a first course, there are many soupy preparations that are served as one-dish meals or as a part of the meal. Both chilled and hot soups, totally vegetarian or made with chunks of fish, chicken, or lamb, are popular. These soups are light and fragrant and stimulate the appetite.

A great thing about these appetizers and soups is that they can be made in advance and briefly heated before serving. Most of them also freeze well. Just remember to serve them all in small portions as they are meant to awaken rather than satisfy the appetite.

Appetizers and Soups

BENGAL FISH BALLS WITH SCALLIONS *MACHI KOFTA*	14
SHRIMP MADRAS *JHEENGA CHAT*	15
SPICY ALMONDS *BHONE BADAAM*	16
LENTIL WAFERS *PUPPADUM/PAPAD*	17
CAULIFLOWER AND PEANUT FRITTERS *GOBHI PAKORA*	18
FRAGRANT ONION AND ZUCCHINI FRITTERS *PIAZ GHIA PAKORA*	19
POTATO AND EGGPLANT FRITTERS *ALOO PAKORA*	20
SPINACH FRITTERS *PALAK PAKORA*	21
PAPAYA AND POTATO SALAD *PAPEETA ALOO CHAT*	22
MULLIGATAWNY *MOLAHATANNI*	23
CHICKEN STOCK *YAKHNI*	25
INDIAN CHICKEN SOUP *MURGH SHORVA*	26
BANGALORE PEANUT SOUP *MOONGPHALI SHORVA*	27
NEW DELHI VEGETARIAN VEGETABLE SOUP *SABZI SHORVA*	28
ICED YOGURT SOUP WITH MINT *DAHI SHORVA*	29

BENGAL FISH BALLS
with Scallions

Machi Kofta

A specialty of Bangladesh, these little balls are delicious served as an appetizer with a dipping sauce such as Mint Chutney (page 159). They also make a fine light meal accompanied by a salad.

SERVES 6

3/4 pound skinless and boneless sole, flounder, scrod, or haddock fillets, poached and flaked

1 pound potatoes, boiled, peeled, and coarsely mashed

1/4 cup plain yogurt

1/2 cup thinly sliced scallions, both white and green parts

1 tablespoon finely chopped fresh ginger

2 teaspoons lemon juice

1 tablespoon Curry Powder (page 6)

2 teaspoons dry mustard

1 teaspoon coarse salt

Peanut or corn oil, for deep-frying

1. Combine all the ingredients except the oil in a bowl and mix well. Pick up the mixture in 1-tablespoonful amounts and roll into neat balls. You should have about 36 balls.

2. Pour the oil into a *karhai* or deep-fryer to a depth of 2 inches. Heat over medium-high heat to 375°. When the oil is hot, slip in a few balls at a time, making sure not to overcrowd the pan. Fry the balls, turning, until golden brown and crisp all around, about 4 minutes. Using a slotted spoon, remove and drain on paper towels. *(The balls may be made ahead and refrigerated for up to 4 hours. To reheat, drop them into hot oil for 45 seconds and serve. Or reheat in a 325° oven for 7 minutes.)*

3. Serve immediately.

Variation

Cooked minced shrimp, scallops, or chicken breast meat may be used instead of the fish.

SHRIMP MADRAS

Jheenga Chat

Here is a wonderful recipe of the chettinad *(business community) of Madras, whose food often reflects a fusion of northern and southern flavors. In this shrimp preparation, for example, both Curry Powder and* Garam Masala *are used to achieve intriguingly complex results.*

SERVES 4

1¹/₂ pounds jumbo or large shrimp, peeled, deveined, and rinsed

1 teaspoon Curry Powder (page 6)

1 teaspoon *Garam Masala* (page 7)

24 fresh kari leaves, cut into chiffonade, or 1 tablespoon dried kari leaves, coarsely powdered

1 teaspoon minced garlic

1 tablespoon vegetable oil

1 tablespoon tomato paste

¹/₄ cup coconut milk, fresh (see page 179) or canned

Coarse salt

1 tablespoon lemon juice

1 (6- to 7-ounce) bunch watercress, trimmed, rinsed, and patted dry

1. Place the shrimp in a bowl. Add the Curry Powder, *Garam Masala*, kari leaves, garlic, and oil and toss well.

2. Heat a frying pan over high heat until very hot. Add the shrimp and sear, shaking and tossing, for 1 minute, or until they begin to turn pink and curl up. Whisk the tomato paste into the coconut milk and add to the pan. Continue to cook until the sauce is reduced to a glaze and the shrimp are cooked through, about 5 minutes. Sprinkle with salt to taste and lemon juice and turn off the heat.

3. Spread the watercress on a plate and mound the shrimp on top of it. Serve immediately.

Variation

For a hotter tasting dish, add 1 teaspoon cracked black peppercorns or 3/4 teaspoon crushed red pepper flakes.

SPICY ALMONDS

Bhone Badaam

BEWARE: *These addictive nibbles go very fast and can easily ruin the appetite for good things to come. In this recipe, the heat is moderate. For a spicier version, increase the ground red pepper to 2 tablespoons.*

SERVES 8

2 teaspoons ground cumin

2 teaspoons ground red pepper

1 teaspoon coarse salt

$^{1}/_{2}$ cup vegetable oil

16 ounces (about 3 cups) whole unblanched almonds

$^{1}/_{4}$ cup water

2 teaspoons lemon juice

$^{1}/_{4}$ cup sugar

1. Combine the cumin, red pepper, and salt in a small bowl. Set aside.

2. Heat the oil over medium heat in a *karhai* or large skillet. Add the almonds and fry, stirring constantly, until the nuts are puffed and give off a roasted fragrance, about 5 minutes. Do not overfry, or they will taste burned. Drain the nuts in a sieve and set aside.

3. Heat the water, lemon juice, and sugar in a small pot over medium heat until the sugar is completely dissolved. Increase the heat and boil the syrup rapidly for 3 minutes. Turn off the heat. Add the nuts and mix well to coat. Spread the nuts in a single layer on a baking sheet. Immediately sprinkle them with the spice mixture, turning to coat evenly.

4. Cool completely before serving.

Variation

Substitute 16 ounces (about 3 cups) raw cashews or shelled walnuts for the almonds.

LENTIL WAFERS

Puppadum/Papad

These ready-made dried lentil wafers come in such flavors as garlic, black pepper, and cumin. All you need to do is dip them in hot oil; they will puff up and cook in a matter of seconds. Two or three per person is a good portion size. To add a delicious crunch to a salad, crumble the puppadum *and sprinkle over as a topping.*

SERVES 8

Peanut or corn oil, for deep-frying

1 package storebought
puppadum/papad

1. Pour the oil into a *karhai* or a deep-fryer to a depth of 2 inches. Heat over medium-high heat to 375°.

2. When the oil is hot, slip 1 wafer into the oil. Fry for about 5 seconds, or until the wafer turns several shades lighter and expands considerably. Remove with tongs and drain on paper towels. Fry all the wafers the same way.

3. Serve immediately.

NOTE: The *puppadum* can also be baked in a preheated 425° oven for 6 minutes or in the microwave on high for 50 seconds. To reheat *puppadum*, place them in a preheated 350° oven for 5 minutes.

CAULIFLOWER AND PEANUT FRITTERS

Gobhi Pakora

Crunchy and studded with peanuts, these fritters are popular with all age groups, and are great served with a yogurt salad or chutney as a dipping sauce.

SERVES 4

1 (1¹/₂-pound) head cauliflower

Peanut or corn oil, for deep-frying

CHICKPEA BATTER

1 cup chickpea flour

¹/₂ cup finely chopped peanuts

¹/₂ cup chopped cilantro leaves and tender stems

1 tablespoon ground coriander

¹/₂ teaspoon cracked black peppercorns

1 tablespoon peanut or corn oil

¹/₂ cup water

¹/₂ teaspoon baking powder

Coarse salt

1. Trim the cauliflower and cut into florets. Pour the oil into a *karhai* or a deep-fryer to a depth of 2¹/₂ inches. Heat over medium-high heat to 375°.

2. Combine all the ingredients for the batter, including salt to taste, in a large bowl and mix thoroughly to make a smooth batter. Add the cauliflower florets, turning to coat evenly.

3. Add the cauliflower, a few pieces at a time, to the hot oil. Do not overcrowd the pan. Fry until the coating is golden brown, turning occasionally, about 6 minutes. Remove with a slotted spoon and drain on paper towels. *(The fritters may be made ahead and refrigerated for up to 1 day or frozen. Defrost frozen fritters before refrying. Reheat the fritters in hot oil for 30 seconds, or reheat frozen fritters in a 375° oven for 10 minutes.)*

4. Serve immediately.

Variation

Substitute the same amount of broccoli, trimmed, peeled, and cut into 1-inch pieces, for the cauliflower.

FRAGRANT ONION
and Zucchini Fritters

Piaz Ghia Pakora

These fritters, scented with cumin and coriander, are a popular North Indian snack. They are excellent served with drinks or afternoon tea. Their versatile flavor makes it possible to serve them before any main dish.

SERVES 4

Peanut or corn oil, for deep-frying

4 onions, peeled and
    thinly sliced

1 small zucchini, grated

1 lightly packed cup cilantro leaves
    and tender stems

¹/4 cup yogurt

1 cup chickpea flour or all-purpose
    flour

2 teaspoons ground cumin

¹/2 teaspoon ground red pepper

1 teaspoon baking powder

Coarse salt

1. Pour the oil into a *karhai* or deep-fryer to a depth of 2 inches. Heat over medium-high heat to 375°.

2. Put all the remaining ingredients, including salt to taste, in a bowl and mix until the vegetables are evenly coated. Gently drop the batter mixture, in 2-tablespoonful amounts, into the oil. Make only a few fritters at a time, so that there is ample room for them to float easily in the oil. Fry the fritters, turning them until they are golden brown all over, 8 to 10 minutes. Remove with a slotted spoon and drain on paper towels. *(The fritters may be made ahead and refrigerated for up to 1 day or frozen. Defrost frozen fritters before refrying. Reheat the fritters in hot oil for 30 seconds, or reheat frozen fritters in a 375° oven for 10 minutes.)*

3. Serve immediately.

Variation

Substitute 8 ounces asparagus, trimmed, peeled, and sliced into 1-inch pieces, for the zucchini. Increase yogurt to ¹/2 cup.

POTATO AND EGGPLANT FRITTERS

Aloo Pakora

These fritters are popular throughout India, where the flavoring varies from region to region. In North India, for example, Garam Masala is a favorite flavoring while Curry Powder is more common in the south. Onions, zucchini, or cauliflower are often substituted for the eggplant. Follow these spicy fritters with an earthy and smoky dish like Tandoori Chicken (page 70).

SERVES 4

3/4 pound small waxy new potatoes

1 small eggplant (about 3/4 pound)

BATTER

1 1/2 cups chickpea flour

1 tablespoon vegetable oil

1 cup water

1 tablespoon lemon juice

1 tablespoon *Garam Masala* (page 7) or Curry Powder (page 6)

1 teaspoon baking soda

1 teaspoon coarse salt

Peanut or corn oil, for deep-frying

1. Scrub the potatoes and cut them into $1/8$-inch-thick rounds. Quarter the eggplant lengthwise and cut it crosswise into $1/4$-inch-thick slices. Put the vegetables in a bowl of water and set aside.

2. Combine all the ingredients for the batter, including salt to taste, in a large bowl and mix thoroughly to make a smooth batter.

3. Pour the oil into a *karhai* or a deep-fryer to a depth of $2 1/2$ inches. Heat over medium-high heat to 375°.

4. Drain the vegetables and lightly pat dry with paper towels. Dip the vegetables into the batter and gently drop into the oil. Make only a few fritters at a time, so that there is ample room for them to float easily in the oil. Fry, turning frequently, until the coating is golden brown, about 7 minutes. Remove with a slotted spoon and drain on paper towels. Serve immediately.

SPINACH FRITTERS

Palak Pakora

Another excellent cocktail-hour nibble, these fritters are lovely made with leaf spinach. Serve them with Peach Chutney with Walnuts and Saffron (page 163).

SERVES 4

8 ounces leaf spinach

BATTER

1 cup chickpea flour

1 tablespoon vegetable oil

2/3 cup water

1 teaspoon minced garlic

2 teaspoons ground coriander

1 teaspoon cumin seeds

1/2 teaspoon crushed red pepper flakes

1/2 teaspoon baking powder

1 teaspoon coarse salt

Peanut or corn oil, for deep-frying

1. Trim and wash the spinach thoroughly and cut any large leaves in half. Combine all the ingredients for the batter, including salt to taste, in a large bowl and mix thoroughly to make a smooth batter.

2. Pour the oil into a *karhai* or deep-fryer to a depth of 2 1/2 inches. Heat over medium-high heat to 375°.

3. When the oil is hot, add the spinach, a few leaves at a time, to the batter, mix to coat, and drop into the hot oil. Do not overcrowd the pan. Fry until golden brown, about 3 minutes. Remove with a slotted spoon and drain on paper towels.

4. Serve immediately.

Variation

For a rustic-looking *pakora,* chop the spinach and fold it into the batter. Gently drop 2-tablespoonful amounts of the batter into the oil and fry. Other greens, such as watercress, arugula, mustard, or kale, may be substituted for the spinach.

PAPAYA AND POTATO SALAD

Papeeta Aloo Chat

A New Delhi specialty, papaya chat is one of my favorite appetizers. Chats are snacks served by street vendors and sidewalk cafes in India. They can be a light meal or side dish and also lend themselves perfectly to picnics or buffets. For a more substantial salad, fold in 8 ounces of cooked chicken, fish, shrimp, or crabmeat. The spices and salt make the fruit sweat, so for best results assemble the chat just before serving.

SERVES 4

1 ripe papaya

1 pound potatoes, boiled, peeled, and cut into $1/4$-inch slices

1 tablespoon maple syrup or honey

$1/4$ cup lemon juice

Coarse salt

2 teaspoons ground toasted cumin seeds

$1/4$ cup finely chopped mint leaves

$1/2$ cup finely chopped cilantro leaves and tender stems

4 green chiles, seeded and sliced

1 teaspoon chopped fresh ginger

2 teaspoons *chat masala* (see Note)

4 lettuce leaves

1. Cut the papaya in half, scoop out the seeds, and peel carefully. Cut each half into 1-inch wedges and put in a bowl. Add all the other ingredients, except the lettuce leaves, and toss well.

2. Arrange the salad on the lettuce leaves on individual plates and serve.

NOTE: *Chat masala,* a packaged blend of such spices as black salt, mango powder, and other digestives, can be purchased at Indian grocery stores.

Variation

Substitute other seasonal fruit for the papaya, such as peaches, apricots, apples, bananas, kiwifruit, and slightly unripe mangoes, or a combination. Or substitute 1 green bell pepper and 1 red bell pepper, seeded and cut into 1-inch squares, for the potatoes and omit the green chiles.

MULLIGATAWNY

Molahatanni

Mulligatawny, a curried meat and vegetable soup, originated in the British Raj. There are as many interpretations of this soup as there are cooks in India. This one is from the Planter's Club in Ootacamund, a small town in southern India. Depending upon how spicy you want the soup to be, add more or less ground red pepper.

SERVES 8

$^1/_3$ cup yellow split peas (see Note)

1 cup chopped carrot

1 cup chopped zucchini

1 cup chopped potato

1 tablespoon chopped fresh ginger

$3^1/_2$ cups Chicken Stock (recipe follows)

$2^1/_2$ cups finely chopped onions

1 lightly packed cup chopped cilantro leaves and tender stems

3 tablespoons *usli ghee* (page 185) or clarified butter

1 tablespoon finely chopped garlic

$^1/_2$ teaspoon ground red pepper

2 tablespoons Curry Powder (page 6)

$^1/_2$ cup heavy or light cream, or milk

1 cup chopped cooked chicken (optional)

Coarse salt and black pepper

1. Pick over the split peas, discarding any shriveled ones or pebbles, rinse, and drain. Put the peas, carrot, zucchini, potato, ginger, stock, 1 cup of the onion, and $^1/_2$ cup of the cilantro in a deep pot and place over high heat. Bring to a boil. Lower the heat and simmer, covered, for 45 minutes, or until the peas are very tender. Let cool. Purée the soup in batches using a blender or food processor. Return the soup to the pot and reheat.

2. Meanwhile, heat the *usli ghee* in a frying pan over medium-high heat. Add the remaining $1^1/_2$ cups onion, the garlic, red pepper, and Curry Powder. Cook, stirring constantly, until the onion is lightly fried, about 6 minutes. Pour the contents of the frying pan into the soup. Stir in the cream and chicken, and season with salt and pepper.

(continued)

23

3. When piping hot, ladle into individual soup bowls. Garnish with the remaining $^1/_2$ cup cilantro. Serve immediately.

NOTE: While it's preferable to use Indian yellow split peas, the dried yellow peas available in supermarkets can be substituted.

Variation

Substitute any cooked seafood, such as crabmeat or lobster, for the chicken.

CHICKEN STOCK

Yakhni

Indian chicken stock is highly fragrant, with cumin, fresh ginger, garlic, and cilantro. The stock is wonderful in soups, pilafs, and curries. It is fairly simple to make: all you do is boil bones in the aromatic liquid. For a spicier stock, add chopped hot green chile.

MAKES ABOUT 4 CUPS

4 cups chicken, duck, or turkey bones, lightly cracked

6 cups water

1 teaspoon cumin seeds

4 cloves garlic, roughly sliced

1 (^{1}/$_2$-inch) piece fresh ginger

1 lightly packed cup cilantro leaves and tender stems

Combine all the ingredients in a deep pot and bring to a boil over high heat. Lower the heat and simmer, uncovered, for 2 hours. Turn off the heat. When cool, strain the stock and use or store in 2-pint containers. *(The stock keeps for 3 days in the refrigerator or up to 3 months in the freezer.)*

Variation

Indian chefs, like Western chefs, are very aware of not wasting scraps of food or discarded produce. You can easily fashion a delicious and healthful vegetarian stock by simmering the leaves, stalks, and trimmings of produce in water with some spices. The stock can be made rich and flavorful by slowly cooking the vegetables and allowing the liquid to reduce by half.

INDIAN CHICKEN SOUP

Murgh Shorva

From the Muslim community in northwestern India, this piquant soup is particularly welcome on a cool winter day. If desired, serve it with crackers alongside.

SERVES 8

1 (3-pound) chicken, quartered

4 tablespoons *usli ghee* (page 185) or vegetable oil

1 tablespoon thinly sliced garlic

2 tablespoons julienned fresh ginger

2 teaspoons *Garam Masala* (page 7) or ground cumin

2 bay leaves

1 1/2 cups thinly sliced onion

3 lemon slices

8 cups water

2 tablespoons finely chopped mint

Coarse salt and black pepper

1 whole lemon, halved

1. Rinse the chicken and pat it dry. Place a heavy, deep pot over medium-high heat and add the *usli ghee* and chicken. Cook until the chicken is lightly seared, about 5 minutes. Add the garlic, ginger, *Garam Masala*, bay leaves, onion, and lemon slices. Cook until the spices give off an aroma.

2. Add the water and bring to a boil. Skim off the scum as it rises to the top. Lower the heat and simmer, partially covered, for 2 to 6 hours (the longer the soup simmers, the richer the flavor will be). Add more water as necessary during cooking. Strain the soup and discard the solids. Stir in the mint and salt and pepper to taste. Add a squeeze of lemon juice to taste.

3. Serve piping hot in mugs.

BANGALORE PEANUT SOUP

Moongphali Shorva

This delicate soup, rich with sweet creamy peanuts and herbal coriander, comes from Bangalore, hometown of the Anglo-Indians.

SERVES 6

2 tablespoons *usli ghee* (page 185) or clarified butter

1 tablespoon ground coriander

$1/2$ teaspoon turmeric

1 teaspoon minced garlic

$1^1/2$ cups finely chopped onion

1 teaspoon ground ginger

4 cups Chicken Stock, homemade (page 25) or canned

$1/2$ cup creamy peanut butter

1 tablespoon sesame paste (optional)

3 tablespoons cornstarch dissolved in $1/4$ cup water

$1/3$ cup heavy or light cream, or milk

Coarse salt and black pepper

2 tablespoons lime juice

Chopped roasted peanuts, chopped scallions, chopped cilantro leaves, and minced green chiles, for garnish

1. Heat the *usli ghee* in a deep pot over medium-high heat. Add the coriander, turmeric, garlic, onion, and ginger. Cook until the onions are lightly fried, about 6 minutes. Add the stock, peanut butter, and sesame paste and bring to a boil. Lower the heat and simmer for 5 minutes.

2. Add the cornstarch mixture and cook, stirring constantly, until the soup thickens, about 2 minutes. Stir in the cream, salt, and a liberal grinding of pepper. Heat until piping hot.

3. Add the lime juice, garnish with peanuts, scallions, cilantro, and chiles, and serve.

NEW DELHI
VEGETARIAN VEGETABLE SOUP

Sabzi Shorva

A popular dish from the Indian capital, this soup is bursting with the flavor of garden-fresh vegetables. It makes a light meal with bread and salad. The soup traditionally has a glowing hot flavor due to the addition of ground hot pepper. For a milder flavor, reduce or eliminate the red pepper.

SERVES 6

1 (2-pound) head cauliflower

2 medium potatoes, peeled and diced

2 cups chopped peeled tomatoes, fresh or canned

1 teaspoon turmeric

1/2 teaspoon ground red pepper

2 tablespoons vegetable oil

1 teaspoon cumin seeds

3 cups water

1 cup frozen peas

Coarse salt and black pepper

1/2 lightly packed cup chopped cilantro leaves and tender stems

1. Trim the cauliflower and cut it into florets. Peel the stems and cut them into small pieces. Combine the cauliflower, potatoes, tomatoes, turmeric, and red pepper in a bowl.

2. Heat the oil in a deep pot over medium-high heat. Add the cumin and cook until the seeds turn dark brown. Add the vegetable-spice mixture and water. Bring to a boil. Lower the heat and simmer, covered, until the vegetables are tender, about 20 minutes. Add the frozen peas and continue to cook for 10 minutes. Season with salt and black pepper.

3. Sprinkle with the chopped cilantro and serve.

ICED YOGURT SOUP WITH MINT

Dahi Shorva

An uncommonly refreshing soup to beat the heat. It is simple and quick to make on hot summer days.

SERVES 4

2 cups yogurt

1 cup buttermilk

$^1/_4$ cup ice water

2 teaspoons honey or sugar

$^1/_2$ teaspoon coarse salt

1 teaspoon ground toasted cumin
  seeds (page 180)

2 tablespoons minced mint

1 cup grated cucumber, drained

$^1/_2$ cup finely diced red bell pepper

$^1/_4$ cup thinly sliced scallions, white
  and green parts

$^1/_2$ cup toasted chopped walnuts or
  cashews

Mint sprigs, for garnish

1. Whisk together the yogurt, buttermilk, ice water, honey, salt, cumin, mint, cucumber, bell pepper, and scallions in a large bowl. Transfer to a chilled soup tureen.

2. Sprinkle with walnuts, garnish with mint sprigs, and serve.

Variations

A nice addition to this soup is seedless green or red grapes—left whole if small or cut in half if large. Lightly toasted chopped pistachio nuts or hazelnuts can be substituted for the walnuts.

BREADS AND
SAVORY PASTRIES

SECOND only to tandoori chicken, Indian breads are the most popular item on an Indian restaurant menu. Made with whole wheat flour and sometimes flavored with spices, herbs, and vegetable purées, these breads are very satisfying. Most are unleavened flatbreads that are easy and quick to make. Those familiar with the Mexican tortilla will find a striking resemblance, except that everyday Indian breads are lighter since they are made with no fat or oil.

All breads may be made ahead and set aside at room temperature or refrigerated until needed, depending on the bread. To reheat, place in a hot frying pan for a few minutes, one at a time. Or heat the entire batch in a preheated 400° oven for 4 minutes or in the microwave for 40 seconds.

GRIDDLE-BAKED FLATBREAD

Chapati

Chapati, *a wholesome and earthy-tasting whole wheat bread, is a staple of North India. Chapatis are similar to flour tortillas except these breads are always made with whole grain flour with the bran and germ intact. The soft and pliable chapati is made by rolling out the dough into a thin round disk and baking it on a hot griddle.* Chapati *goes well with all dishes.*

SERVES 4 TO 6

MAKES 12 *CHAPATIS*

1¹/₂ cups *chapati* flour, or ³/₄ cup whole wheat flour and ³/₄ cup unbleached all-purpose flour, plus additional flour for dusting

¹/₂ cup warm water

3 tablespoons *usli ghee* (page 185) or clarified butter (optional)

1. Put the flour in a large bowl. If using whole wheat and all-purpose flour, stir to combine. Pour the water and 1 tablespoon of the *usli ghee* over the flour. Mix thoroughly until the flour sticks together. Transfer the dough to a lightly floured surface and knead for 3 minutes. Cover the dough and let it rest for 15 minutes. To make the dough in a food processor, put the flour in the workbowl. If using whole wheat and all-purpose flour, run the machine briefly to combine. With the machine running, add the water and 1 tablespoon *usli ghee* through the feed tube and mix until a ball of dough forms on the blade. Process for 50 seconds to knead. *(The dough may be prepared ahead and set aside at room temperature for up to 8 hours or refrigerated for 5 days. Bring the dough to room temperature before using.)*

2. Shape the dough into a rope and cut it into 12 equal portions. Shape each portion into a smooth ball and roll out into a circle, dusting often with flour to prevent sticking. Cover the rounds with a moist towel as you complete rolling them. Do not stack them.

3. Heat a griddle or a frying pan over medium-high heat until very hot. Working with one at a time, place a round on the hot griddle. Bake for 1^1/$_2$ to 2 minutes or until brown spots appear on the underside. Turn the bread using tongs and continue to bake for 1 minute more, or until brown spots appear on the second side.

4. Remove and brush lightly with the remaining 2 tablespoons *usli ghee*.

5. Serve immediately or keep warm, covered, in a low oven.

FLAME-ROASTED PUFFY BREAD

Phulka

In the North Indian language, phulka *means puffed, which is what these balloon-like breads are. Here,* chapatis *are baked for a second time by being toasted over a gas flame or on an electric burner. If you use an electric burner, place a cake rack flat on the burner and turn the temperature to the highest level. You can also toast the breads by placing them briefly on the rack of a preheated charcoal or electric grill. Traditionally* phulkas *are served with a dal. Try them with New Delhi Spiced Lentils (page 148) or Braised Chickpeas with Spicy Sauce (page 145).*

SERVES 4 TO 6
MAKES 12 *PHULKAS*

1 recipe *chapati* (page 32)

3 tablespoons *usli ghee* (page 185) or clarified butter (optional)

1. Make the *chapatis* through step 3 as directed on pages 32 to 33.

2. Pick up a piece of bread with tongs and place it directly over a gas flame or an electric burner. Toast the bread briefly until it is lightly spotted with brown and puffs into a pillow. Turn the bread a few times to ensure even browning and prevent it from burning.

3. Drizzle *usli ghee* on top and serve immediately.

NOTE: These breads are meant to be eaten as soon as they are baked; they deflate with time.

BAKED TANDOORI BREAD

Nan

Nan *is the popular bread generally served in Indian restaurants. It is the obvious choice to accompany tandoori meat, chicken, or vegetables (see chapter on Tandoori Grilling) because it is baked in the* tandoor, *the Indian clay oven, after the meat.*

SERVES 8

MAKES 8 NANS

^{1}/$_2$ cup yogurt

^{3}/$_4$ cup boiling water

1 teaspoon active dry yeast

2 teaspoons sugar

^{3}/$_4$ teaspoon coarse salt

^{1}/$_4$ cup melted unsalted butter, plus additional for brushing

1 large egg

3 cups unbleached all-purpose flour, plus additional for dusting

Vegetable oil as needed

1. Whisk together the yogurt and water in a large bowl. Add the yeast, sugar, salt, butter, and egg and mix thoroughly. Add the flour and mix just until a dough forms (the dough will be very soft and sticky). Wipe your hands clean and oil them generously. Knead the dough in the bowl until smooth and satiny, oiling your fingers if necessary, about 10 minutes. Cover and let the dough rest in a warm place for 4 hours, or until doubled in bulk.

2. Preheat the oven to 500°.

3. Punch down the dough, then knead again for 1 minute. Divide the dough into 8 equal portions and roll out each into a 5-inch round, dusting with flour to prevent sticking. Using your hands, stretch the round into a 5 by 7-inch oval. Arrange in a single layer on baking sheets and bake in the middle level of the oven for 4 ^{1}/$_2$ minutes, or until they begin to puff and brown. Remove and, if desired, grill the *nans* briefly, 15 to 20 seconds, to brown nicely. Brush them with additional melted butter.

4. Arrange the *nan* in a small basket and serve immediately.

GREEN CHILE–CORN BREAD

Molahadu

This fragrant bread, imbued with sweetness of corn and accented with slivers of green chiles, is a specialty of the Guntur chile pickers, one of the many migrant groups of southern India. Made with fresh corn, cumin seeds, and chiles, it makes an incredibly satisfying meal when served with a chutney like Peach Chutney with Walnut and Saffron (page 163) or Garlic-Tomato Chutney (page 161). Molahadu is also great with tandoori grilled dishes.

SERVES 6

MAKES 8 *MOLAHADUS*

1 3/4 cups *chapati* flour, or 3/4 cup whole wheat flour and 1 cup unbleached all-purpose flour, plus additional for dusting

1 1/2 cups corn kernels, fresh or frozen and thawed

1/4 cup water, or more as needed

1/3 cup shredded mild or hot green chiles

1 teaspoon cumin seeds

Coarse salt

6 tablespoon *usli ghee* (page 185) or vegetable oil

1. Put the flour in a large bowl. If using whole wheat and all-purpose flour, stir to combine. Add the corn, water, chiles, cumin, and salt to taste. Blend the mixture until it forms a firm, kneadable mass. Add 2 table-spoons of the *usli ghee*, and more water, as necessary, and knead the dough for 1 minute.

2. Divide the dough into 8 equal portions and shape each into a smooth ball. Roll each ball out into a 6-inch round, dusting often with flour to prevent sticking.

3. Heat a griddle or heavy frying pan over high heat. Lower the heat to medium-high and place 1 bread on the griddle. Cook until the under-side is spotted with brown, about 2 minutes. Turn and cook until the second side is spotted with brown and the bread is cooked through, about 1 minute.

4. Brush the top of each round with the *usli ghee*, flip, and cook for about 1 minute. Then coat the other side with *usli ghee*, flip, and cook for another minute. Remove and keep warm, covered, while you cook the remaining rounds.

5. Serve immediately.

NOTE: For an intense roasted-corn flavor, after cooking the bread on the griddle (step 3), hold it directly over a high flame for few seconds, using tongs, and toast, turning frequently. Do not let it burn. Brush generously with *usli ghee* and serve.

DEEP-FRIED PUFFY BREAD

Poori

Poori dough is dropped into hot oil where it metamorphosizes, reappearing as light, airy puffs of bread. Pooris are called show-off breads because they look and taste so sensational. They are the bread of choice for entertaining. Pooris seem to have a particular affinity with potatoes; try them with Cumin Potatoes (page 141).

SERVES 4

MAKES 8 POORIS

¹/₂ cup *chapati* flour or unbleached all-purpose flour, plus additional for dusting

¹/₂ cup self-rising flour

¹/₃ cup buttermilk

Peanut or corn oil, for deep-frying

1. Combine the *chapati* and self-rising flours in a medium bowl. Mix in the buttermilk. Turn out onto a lightly floured surface and knead for 2 minutes. Cover and let rest for 15 minutes. To make the dough in a food processor, put both flours in the workbowl and run the machine until they are blended. With the machine running, add the buttermilk through the feed tube and mix until a ball of dough forms on the blade. Process the dough for 30 seconds, turning the machine on and off every 5 seconds. Transfer the dough to the work surface and keep covered with a moist towel.

2. Divide the dough into 8 pieces. Take 1 piece and shape it into a smooth ball. Dust generously with flour and roll out to a 5-inch circle. Cover and repeat with the remaining pieces of dough. Do not stack the rounds.

3. Pour the oil into a *karhai* or deep-fryer to a depth of 4 inches. Heat over medium-high heat to 375°. Add 1 round to the oil; it will sink to the bottom. When it starts to rise, gently press it in the center with the back of a slotted spoon until the bread puffs, about 30 seconds. Turn and cook until lightly browned, about 20 seconds. Transfer to paper towels. Keep warm while cooking the remaining *pooris*. Place on a platter and serve immediately.

Green Pea Bread

Hari Poori

Another classic bread from North India, Green Pea Bread is loved by grown-ups and children alike. This emerald green poori is made by enriching the dough with puréed green peas and cilantro. I like to add a little ground black pepper, which seems to bring out the herbal flavor of the peas.

SERVES 4

MAKES 8 *POORIS*

1/2 cup frozen green peas, thawed

1/2 lightly packed cup cilantro leaves and tender stems

1 cup unbleached all-purpose flour, plus additional for dusting

1 tablespoon peanut or corn oil

Coarse salt and black pepper

1/4 cup water

Peanut or corn oil, for deep-frying

1. Put the peas and cilantro into the workbowl of a food processor and process for 30 seconds, or until the peas are puréed. Add the flour, oil, and salt and pepper to taste and process until well blended. With the machine running, add the water through the feed tube, mixing until a ball of dough forms on the blade. Process the dough for 30 seconds, turning the machine on and off every 5 seconds. Transfer the dough to a lightly floured surface and keep covered with a moist towel.

2. Divide the dough in half. Shape each half into a rope and cut into 4 equal portions. Cover with a moist towel. Shape each portion of dough into a smooth ball and roll out to a 3-inch circle, dusting often with flour to prevent sticking. Cover and repeat with the remaining pieces of dough. Do not stack the *pooris.*

3. Pour the oil into a *karhai* or deep-fryer to a depth of 3 inches. Heat over medium-high heat to 375°. Add 1 *poori* to the oil; it will sink to the bottom. When it starts to rise, gently press it in the center with the back of a slotted spoon until the bread puffs, about 30 seconds. Turn and cook

(continued)

39

until lightly browned, about 15 seconds. Using the slotted spoon, transfer the *poori* to paper towels. The bread will be light and puffed up, just like a balloon. Keep warm while cooking the remaining breads.

4. Mound the *pooris* in a large shallow basket and serve immediately.

Variation

Substitute an equal amount of cooked and puréed lima beans or green split peas for the green peas.

SWEET PUMPKIN BREAD

Lal Poori

I grew up eating pooris *like this that were flavored with puréed vegetables. They are lovely by themselves with a cup of coffee; they also go nicely with chicken and meat curries.*

SERVES 8

MAKES 16 *POORIS*

1 cup puréed cooked pumpkin, fresh or canned

1/2 teaspoon *Garam Masala* (page 7) or ground cinnamon

1 tablespoon peanut or corn oil

2 1/4 cups *chapati* flour or unbleached all-purpose flour, plus additional for dusting

Peanut or corn oil, for deep-frying

1. Put the pumpkin, *Garam Masala*, oil, and flour in a large bowl and mix well. Add enough water to make the mixture come together in a non-sticky, kneadable dough. Gather the dough together and knead it until smooth, dusting with flour if it is very sticky. To make the dough in a food processor, put the pumpkin, *Garam Masala*, oil, and flour in the workbowl and run the machine until well blended. With the machine running, add water through the feed tube and mix until a ball of dough forms on the blade. Process the dough for 30 seconds, turning the machine on and off every 5 seconds. Transfer the dough to a lightly floured surface and keep covered with a moist towel.

2. Divide the dough in half. Shape each half into a rope and cut into 8 equal portions. Cover with a moist towel. Shape each portion of dough into a smooth ball and roll out to a 3-inch circle, dusting often with flour to prevent sticking. Cover and repeat with the remaining pieces of dough. Do not stack the *pooris*.

3. Pour the oil into a *karhai* or deep-fryer to a depth of 3 inches. Heat over medium-high heat to 375°. Add 1 *poori* to the oil; it will sink to the bottom.

(continued)

41

When it starts to rise, gently press it in the center with the back of a slotted spoon until the bread puffs, about 30 seconds. Turn and cook until lightly browned, about 15 seconds. Using a slotted spoon, transfer to paper towels. The bread will be light and puffed up, just like a balloon. Keep warm while cooking the remaining breads.

4. Mound the *pooris* in a large shallow basket and serve immediately.

Variation

Substitute an equal amount of mashed potato, sweet potato, or turnip for the pumpkin.

FLAKY PARSLEY PINWHEEL BREAD

Saag Paratha

Flavored with the highly aromatic parsley called bandhana, *this bread is among my favorites. In the western province of Punjab in North India, where this bread comes from, parsley is used not as a seasoning herb but as a green, much the way spinach, mustard, and Swiss chard are used. Cut into wedges, parsley bread makes an excellent appetizer with before-dinner drinks. It also goes well with tandoori grilled meats.*

SERVES 4 TO 8

MAKES 8 PARATHAS

1 1/2 cups *chapati* flour, or 3/4 cup whole wheat flour and 3/4 cup unbleached all-purpose flour, plus additional for dusting

1/2 teaspoon nigella or fennel seeds

1/2 teaspoon coarse salt

1/3 cup *usli ghee* (page 185) or vegetable oil

1/2 cup warm water

2 lightly packed cups parsley leaves, minced

1. Put the flour in a large bowl. If using whole wheat and all-purpose flour, stir to combine. Add the nigella, salt, and 1 tablespoon of the *usli ghee*. Add the water and mix until the flour comes together into a non-sticky, kneadable dough. Transfer the dough to a lightly floured work surface and knead for 3 minutes. Cover the dough and let it rest for 15 minutes. To make the dough in a food processor, put the flour in the workbowl. If using whole wheat and all-purpose flour, run the machine briefly to combine. Add the nigella, salt, and 1 tablespoon of the *usli ghee*. With the machine running, add the water through the feed tube and mix until a ball of dough forms on the blade. Process for 50 seconds to knead. *(The dough may be prepared ahead and set aside at room temperature for up to 8 hours or refrigerated for 2 days. Bring the dough to room temperature before using.)*

2. Shape the dough into a ball and roll out to an 8-inch circle, dusting often with flour to prevent sticking. Combine the parsley with 2 tablespoons

(continued)

usli ghee and spread on top of the dough. Roll into a jelly roll and cut the dough into 8 equal portions. Place a portion, cut side up, on a lightly floured surface and roll out to a 5- to 6-inch circle, dusting often with flour. Repeat with the remaining portions, covering the rounds with a moist towel as you complete rolling them. Do not stack them.

3. Heat a griddle or frying pan over medium-high heat until very hot. Place a *paratha* on the griddle and let it cook for 2 to 3 minutes on each side, or until flecked with brown. Pour 2 teaspoons of *usli ghee* on and around the *paratha*. Fry, turning, until it develops patches of brown on each side, about 2 minutes. Remove the bread and keep warm. Cook all the breads the same way.

4. Arrange *parathas* in a small basket and serve immediately.

MOGHUL BREAD
with Fragrant Meat Stuffing

Keema Bhara Paratha

These meat-stuffed breads, fragrant with the characteristic Moghul spices, are a popular Sunday brunch item for people in northern India. They are typically served with a cool yogurt salad, such as Banana-Coconut Yogurt Salad (page 155), an herbal chutney like Mint Chutney (page 159), and Spiced Tea (page 175). I also find these parathas *delicious by themselves, particularly when cut into wedges and served with cocktails.*

SERVES 6

MAKES 6 PARATHAS

1 recipe *chapati* (page 32)

1 recipe Dry-Cooked Spicy Ground
   Beef (page 125)

3 tablespoons vegetable oil

1. Make the *chapati* dough through step 1 as directed on page 32. Divide the dough into 6 equal portions. Divide the beef into 6 portions.

2. Shape 1 piece of dough into a smooth ball. Keep the remainder covered. Roll out the ball of dough on a lightly floured surface to an 8-inch circle, dusting often with flour. Spread 1 portion of meat filling on top. Fold the edges into the center to form a 4-inch circle, pleating and lightly pressing them to seal. Cover with a moist towel. Repeat with the remaining dough and filling. Do not stack the *parathas*.

3. Heat a griddle or frying pan over medium-high heat. Heat $1/2$ teaspoon of the oil and add 1 *paratha*. Cook until it is lightly fried and spotted brown, turning a few times, about 2 minutes. Remove and keep warm. Cook the other *parathas* in the same way.

4. Arrange *parathas* in a basket and serve immediately.

SPICY POTATO-STUFFED BREAD

Aloo Paratha

With a raita salad, this earthy and very satisfying farm-style bread with a spicy potato filling is a meal in one. For a more substantial meal, serve the parathas with a vegetable dish.

SERVES 6

MAKES 6 *PARATHAS*

1 pound potatoes, boiled, peeled, and mashed

1 teaspoon ground coriander

1/4 cup minced cilantro leaves and tender stems

1/2 teaspoon ground red pepper

Coarse salt

1 recipe *chapati* (page 32)

6 tablespoons vegetable oil

1. Combine the potatoes, coriander, cilantro, red pepper, and salt to taste in a bowl and mix well.

2. Follow the directions for *keema bhara paratha* on page 45, using this potato filling instead of the meat filling.

3. Arrange *parathas* on a platter and serve immediately.

TANDOORI BREAD STUFFED
with Cherries and Pistachios

Moghul Nan

A real treat for those who like bread with dried fruits and nuts. This nan *is fine served on its own, but it is really wonderful with tandoori kebabs such as Chicken Ginger Kebabs (page 72) or Spice-Rubbed Grilled Lamb (page 81).*

SERVES 8
MAKES 8 NANS

1 recipe *nan* (page 35)
$^1/_4$ cup chopped dried cherries

$^1/_4$ cup chopped toasted pistachios

Prepare the *nan* dough, kneading the cherries and pistachios into the dough before dividing the dough and rolling it. Make the bread as directed on page 35.

SAVORY PASTRIES
with Spicy Chicken Filling

Murgh Samosa

Samosas *are classic Indian fare—little pastries with a variety of savory stuffings. They make a terrific appetizer for a special dinner party or, served with a salad, a light entrée for family meals.*

SERVES 6
MAKES 12 SAMOSAS

SPICY CHICKEN FILLING

1¹/₂ tablespoons *usli ghee* (page 185) or clarified butter

1 teaspoon minced garlic

1 cup chopped scallions, white and green parts

1 baking potato, boiled, peeled, and cubed

³/₄ pound boneless and skinless chicken breast, cubed

¹/₂ cup peeled and finely grated carrot

2 teaspoons *Garam Masala* (page 7)

Coarse salt

2 teaspoons lemon juice

SAMOSA **DOUGH**

1¹/₂ cups all-purpose flour, plus additional flour for dusting

¹/₄ teaspoon nigella seeds, or ¹/₂ teaspoon dried oregano (optional)

¹/₈ teaspoon baking soda

6 tablespoons warm water

3 tablespoons melted *usli ghee* (page 185) or clarified butter

2 tablespoons plain yogurt

¹/₂ teaspoon coarse salt

Cornstarch, for dusting

2 tablespoons cornstarch dissolved in 3 tablespoons water

Peanut or corn oil, for deep-frying

1. To prepare the filling, heat a large frying pan over medium-high heat. Add the *usli ghee*, garlic, scallions, potato, chicken, and carrot. Cook, stirring occasionally, for 7 minutes, or until lightly fried. Stir in the *Garam Masala*, salt to taste, and lemon juice. Remove from the heat and allow to cool. *(The*

filling may be prepared 1 day ahead. Cover and refrigerate. Bring to room temperature before using.)

2. To prepare the dough, combine the flour, nigella, and baking soda in a large bowl. Whisk together the water, *usli ghee*, yogurt, and salt in a measuring cup until blended. Add to the dry ingredients and stir until the dough comes together. Gather into a ball. Turn the dough out onto a floured work surface and knead until elastic, about 5 minutes. *(The dough may be prepared 1 day ahead. Wrap tightly and refrigerate. Bring to room temperature before continuing.)*

3. Line a baking sheet with plastic wrap, dust lightly with cornstarch, and set aside. Divide the dough into 6 pieces. Shape each piece into a ball. Place 1 ball between the palms of your hands and press to flatten to a 3-inch round. Place on a floured work surface. Using a rolling pin, roll out to a 6-inch round, lifting and turning frequently and dusting the work surface with flour as necessary to prevent sticking. Cut the round in half. Brush half of each straight edge with the cornstarch mixture. Form a cone by folding the second half of the straight edge over the first half and pinch the seam to seal. Hold the cone with the open end up. Stuff with $^1/_4$ cup of the filling. Brush 1 side of the open end with the cornstarch mixture. Pinch the open sides together to enclose the filling. Place the *samosa* on the baking sheet and refrigerate. Repeat with remaining dough balls, cornstarch mixture, and filling.

4. Pour the oil into a *karhai* or a deep-fryer to a depth of 3 inches. Heat over medium-high heat to 375°. Add some *samosas* without crowding and cook until golden, turning occasionally, about 4 minutes. Using a slotted spoon, transfer to paper towels; repeat with remaining *samosas*. *(The* samosas *may be made ahead and refrigerated for up to 2 days. To reheat, slip them into hot oil and fry for 90 seconds or spread them in a single layer on a baking sheet and place in a preheated 350° oven for 10 minutes.)*

5. Mound the *samosas* in a small, shallow basket and serve immediately.

SAVORY PASTRIES
with Spicy Vegetable Filling

Aloo Samosa

Similar to the murgh samosas *(page 48), these have a vegetable filling. Potatoes and peas, spiced with cumin, coriander, paprika, and chiles, make a flavorful stuffing. Serve these* samosas *with Mint Chutney (page 159).*

SERVES 6
MAKES 12 *SAMOSAS*

SPICY VEGETABLE FILLING

1 tablespoon *usli ghee* (page 185) or clarified butter

2 teaspoons cumin seeds

1 tablespoon ground coriander

1 teaspoon minced fresh chiles

2 teaspoons paprika

3 baking potatoes, boiled, peeled, and cubed

1/2 cup frozen green peas, thawed

Coarse salt

1/2 cup chopped cilantro leaves and tender stems

1 recipe *samosa* dough (page 48)

1. To prepare the filing, heat the *usli ghee* in a large frying pan over medium-high heat and add the cumin seeds. When the cumin gets a little darker, add the coriander, chiles, paprika, and potatoes. Cook for 5 minutes, then stir in the peas, salt to taste, and cilantro. Remove from heat and allow to cool. *(The filling may be prepared 1 day ahead. Cover and refrigerate. Bring to room temperature before using.)*

2. To make the *samosas*, prepare the dough, fill the half-rounds, and fry as directed in steps 2, 3, and 4 on page 49. *(The* samosas *may be made ahead and kept refrigerated for up to 4 days. To reheat, slip them into hot oil and fry for 90 seconds or spread them in a single layer on a baking sheet and place in a preheated 350° oven for 10 minutes.)*

3. Mound the *samosas* in a small, shallow basket and serve immediately.

Savory Pastries
with Coconut, Jaggery, and Chile Filling

Mava Samosa

The Gujaratis on the west coast of India have a fondness for combining the four elements of taste: sweet, sour, savory, and hot. Snacks called HotMix and Chivdos, which incorporate such elements, are popular in the region. These sweetish hot pastries make a lovely teatime snack. Serve them hot or at room temperature.

SERVES 6
MAKES 12 *SAMOSAS*

COCONUT, JAGGERY, AND
CHILE FILLING

1 1/2 cups sweetened coconut flakes

1 cup finely chopped pecans

1 tablespoon *usli ghee* (page 185)

2 tablespoons quick-cooking or
regular Cream of Wheat

1/2 cup water

2 teaspoons lemon juice

1/2 cup jaggery or light brown sugar

1/2 cup golden raisins

2 to 4 green chiles, stemmed and
thinly sliced

1 teaspoon ground cardamom

1/4 teaspoon coarse salt

1 recipe *samosa* dough (page 48)

1. Toast the coconut flakes in a dry frying pan over medium heat, turning and tossing until caramel brown, about 7 minutes. Transfer to a plate. Add the pecans to the pan and toast, stirring, until aromatic, about 3 minutes. Add the *usli ghee* and Cream of Wheat to the pan. Cook over medium-high heat, stirring, until the Cream of Wheat is lightly fried, about 2 minutes.

2. Add the water, lemon juice, jaggery, raisins, chiles, cardamom, and salt. Cook until the mixture thickens, about 2 minutes. Fold in the coconut and turn off the heat. Allow to cool.

3. To make the *samosas*, prepare the dough, fill the half-rounds, and fry as directed in steps 2, 3, and 4 on page 49.

4. Mound the *samosas* in a small, shallow basket and serve immediately.

RICE
AND GRAINS

THE Indian long-grain rice called basmati, with its nutty fragrance, milky flavor, and exquisite texture, is unmatched in the world. This is the rice that is commonly used in Indian pilafs and the baked rice dish called biriyani. The rice is cooked with other ingredients such as fruits, herbs, and highly aromatic spices, such as cinnamon, cardamom, cloves, bay leaves, and cumin. The spices are usually added whole so as not to alter the glossy appearance and pure color of the rice. While cinnamon may be left as a garnish, bay leaves, cardamom pods, and cloves must be removed and discarded, even though no harm is caused by accidentally biting into one. Basmati rice is widely available, so do try to get it; there is really no good substitute. If necessary, however, you may substitute jasmine rice (another scented long-grain rice from Asia), regular long-grain rice, or converted (parboiled) rice. In addition to white rice, pilafs are made with brown basmati, Cream of Rice, flaked rice, semolina (Cream of Wheat is a good substitute), cracked wheat, millet, and barley.

Three Ways to Cook Perfect Basmati Rice

Each of these techniques produces perfectly cooked basmati rice.

- The first technique is the one I introduced in 1983 while I was executive chef at an Indian restaurant. It is similar to cooking pasta. The rice is cooked in a large quantity of boiling water, then drained and served.

- The second technique is the one I learned at my mother's side in her kitchen in New Delhi; it is the classic steaming method. The rice is cooked in exactly twice the amount of water. It is first boiled, then steamed until fully cooked.

- In the third technique, known as the Moghul method, the rice is first boiled rapidly in a large quantity of water until partially cooked, then baked in the oven.

Regardless of the cooking process, basmati rice is always rinsed thoroughly and soaked in cold water for thirty minutes before cooking to permit the grains to expand better. Basmati grains are thinner than other rice grains; they have a loose inner structure and are low in starch. So soaking softens and relaxes the grains, thus reducing the amount of liquid needed and the cooking time.

Cooked basmati may be kept, covered, at room temperature for up to eight hours or refrigerated for two days. Reheat the rice in a frying pan over medium heat, stirring carefully, until heated through, or place in a preheated 350° oven, wrapped in foil, for fifteen minutes. If the rice looks dry, sprinkle a tablespoon or two of water over it before heating.

To reheat in a microwave, place rice in a microwave-safe dish, cover, and heat at 100 percent power. Four cups of cooked rice will take four minutes to reheat.

PERFECT BOILED BASMATI RICE

Obla Chawal

SERVES 4

1¹/₂ cups basmati rice

1. Rinse the rice thoroughly in several changes of cold water and put it in a bowl. Add enough cold water to cover the rice by 1 inch. Soak the rice for at least 30 minutes or up to 2 hours. Drain the rice.

2. While the rice is soaking, bring a large quantity of water, about 8 cups, to a boil in a deep pot. Add the drained rice and bring back to a boil, stirring occasionally with a fork to ensure that the rice does not settle at the bottom of the pan. Cook for exactly 4 minutes. Remove from the heat and drain well.

3. Transfer the rice to a heated platter and serve immediately.

NOTE: If not serving immediately, drizzle 1 teaspoon *usli ghee* (page 185) or vegetable oil over the rice, gently folding it in. Cover and set aside until ready to use.

PERFECT STEAMED BASMATI RICE

Bhapa Chawal

SERVES 4

1¹/₂ cups basmati rice

1. Rinse the rice in several changes of cold water and put it in a heavy saucepan. Add 3 cups cold water. Soak the rice for at least 30 minutes or up to 2 hours.

2. Place the saucepan with the rice and water over high heat and bring to a boil, stirring occasionally with a fork to ensure that the rice does not settle at the bottom of the pan. Decrease the heat to medium and cook the rice, partially covered, until most of the water is absorbed and the surface of the rice is covered with steam holes, about 8 minutes.

3. Cover the pan tightly and decrease the heat as low as possible. Let the rice steam for 10 minutes. Remove from the heat and let the rice rest, covered and undisturbed, for 5 minutes before serving. Fluff with a fork.

4. Transfer to a heated platter and serve immediately.

PERFECT BAKED BASMATI RICE

Dum Chawal

SERVES 4

1¹/₂ cups basmati rice

1 tablespoon *usli ghee* (page 185) or clarified butter

1. Rinse the rice in several changes of cold water and put it in a heavy saucepan. Add 3 cups cold water. Soak the rice for at least 30 minutes or up to 2 hours, then drain.

2. While the rice is soaking, preheat the oven to 325°.

3. Bring a large quantity of water, about 8 cups, to a boil in a deep pot. Add the drained rice and bring back to a boil, stirring occasionally with a fork to ensure that the rice does not settle at the bottom of the pan. Cook for exactly 2¹/₂ minutes. Drain the rice and put it in an ovenproof casserole with a lid. Add the *usli ghee*, mix carefully, cover, and bake on the middle rack for 25 minutes. Turn off the oven and let the rice rest, covered and undisturbed, for 10 minutes. Fluff with a fork.

4. Transfer to a heated platter and serve immediately.

LEMON PILAF

Chitrannam

A subtly flavored and visually appealing lemon rice from South India brings forth the very essence of Indian summer. It is a good pilaf to serve with steamed and grilled fish and shellfish such as Steamed Fish in Herb Sauce (page 90) or Parsi Breaded Shrimp in Green Paste (page 99).

SERVES 4

1 tablespoon vegetable oil

1 teaspoon mustard seeds

$^1/_4$ teaspoon asafetida, or $^1/_2$ teaspoon minced garlic

$^1/_2$ teaspoon turmeric

$1^1/_2$ tablespoons lemon juice

3 tablespoons water

$2^1/_2$ cups cooked rice made with 1 cup raw rice (basmati, brown rice, or converted rice)

$^1/_4$ cup chopped roasted cashews

Coarse salt

$^1/_2$ teaspoon minced green chiles (optional)

12 kari leaves, fresh or dried (optional)

1 firm, ripe mango, peeled, pitted, and diced into $^1/_2$-inch pieces, for garnish (optional)

1. Heat the oil in a heavy saucepan over medium-high heat. When the oil is hot, add the mustard seeds and cover the pan with the lid because the seeds will pop and spatter. When the spluttering subsides, add the asafetida, turmeric, lemon juice, and water and bring to a boil.

2. Stir in the rice, cashews, salt to taste, chiles, and kari leaves. Toss well until the rice is evenly seasoned.

3. Serve hot, at room temperature, or cold, garnished with mango.

PEACH AND WALNUT BASMATI PILAF

Khoobani Pulao

Fruit pilaf is a classic Moghul creation and this peach pilaf is one of the best. The combination of fruit and nuts with the fragrant rice provides a truly sensuous experience. It is perfect with Tandoori Chicken (page 70) or Malabar Coconut Shrimp (page 98).

SERVES 6

1¹/₂ cups basmati rice

3 cups peaches, peeled and sliced

¹/₂ teaspoon ground ginger

¹/₂ teaspoon ground fennel

¹/₄ teaspoon grated nutmeg

2 tablespoons *usli ghee* (page 185) or clarified butter

¹/₃ cup walnut pieces

1. Rinse the rice in several changes of cold water and put in a bowl. Add enough cold water to cover the rice by 1 inch. Soak the rice for at least 30 minutes or up to 2 hours. Drain.

2. Combine 1 cup of the peach slices and 1 cup water in a food processor and process until the fruit is liquefied. Add enough water to make 3 cups peach juice. Stir in the ginger, fennel, and nutmeg.

3. Transfer the spiced peach juice to a heavy saucepan. Add the rice and bring to a boil, stirring occasionally with a fork to ensure that the rice does not settle at the bottom of the pan. Decrease the heat to medium and cook, partially covered, for 8 minutes for basmati rice (13 minutes for regular rice), or until most of the water is absorbed and the surface of the rice is covered with several steam holes. Cover the pan tightly and decrease the heat as low as possible. Let the rice steam for 10 minutes. Remove from the heat and let the rice rest, covered and undisturbed, for 5 minutes.

4. Heat the *usli ghee* in a frying pan and add the walnuts. Fry the nuts, shaking and stirring, for 1 minute. Add the remaining 2 cups peaches and cook until the fruit is warmed through and glazed, about 2 minutes. Serve the pilaf garnished with peach slices and walnuts.

ORANGE-CINNAMON BASMATI PILAF

Naarangi Pulao

This is a highly aromatic citrus-sweet pilaf that showcases the beautiful flavor of the basmati rice. Because of its keeping quality, orange-cinnamon pilaf is perfect for picnics or buffet tables. This pilaf is totally salt- and fat-free. Serve the pilaf with Country Captain (page 108) or Malabar Coconut Shrimp (page 98).

SERVES 4

1 cup brown basmati or regular brown rice

3/4 cup orange juice

1 (3-inch) stick cinnamon

5 whole cloves

1/2 teaspoon grated fresh ginger

1/4 cup dark raisins

Orange slices, for garnish (optional)

1. Rinse the rice well with cold water and place in a bowl. Add 1 1/2 cups cold water and let soak for at least 30 minutes or up to 2 hours. Drain the rice, reserving the water.

2. Place a saucepan over high heat. Add all the other ingredients, including the reserved water, except the orange slices, and bring to a boil. Decrease the heat to medium. Add the rice to the saucepan. Cook, partially covered, for 15 minutes for basmati rice (18 minutes for regular rice), or until most of the moisture is absorbed and the surface of the rice is covered with steam holes. Cover the pan tightly and decrease the heat as low as possible.

3. Let the rice steam for 10 minutes. Remove from the heat and let the rice rest, covered, for 5 minutes. Remove the cinnamon stick and cloves and fluff with a fork.

4. Transfer to a heated platter, garnish with orange slices, and serve.

GREEN PEA PILAF

Matar Pulao

This pearl-white pilaf, studded with forest green peas, is a Moghul classic. Because of its subtle, mellow flavor, it is the most popular rice pilaf at Indian restaurants. The pilaf can be cooked either in a rich chicken stock or plain water. It is wonderful both ways.

SERVES 4

1¹/₂ cups basmati or regular long-grain rice

2 tablespoons vegetable oil

¹/₂ teaspoon cumin seeds

4 green whole cardamom pods

2 whole cloves

1 bay leaf

¹/₂ cup chopped onion

¹/₂ teaspoon ground ginger

3 cups Chicken Stock (page 25) or water

Coarse salt

1 (10-ounce) package frozen green peas, thawed

1. Rinse the rice well with cold water and put it in a bowl. Add cold water to cover the rice by 1 inch and soak for at least 30 minutes or up to 2 hours. Drain.

2. Heat the oil in a saucepan over medium-high heat. When the oil is hot, add the cumin, cardamom, cloves, and bay leaf. When the cumin turns several shades darker, add the onion. Cook until the onion begins to brown, about 5 minutes. Add the rice, ginger, stock, and salt to taste and bring to a boil. Decrease the heat to medium and cook, partially covered, for 8 minutes for basmati rice (12 minutes for regular rice), or until most of the liquid is absorbed and the surface of the rice is covered with steam holes. Cover the pan, and decrease the heat to low.

3. Let the rice steam for 10 minutes. Remove from the heat, stir in the peas, and let the rice rest, covered, for 5 minutes. Remove the cardamom, cloves, and bay leaf and fluff the rice with a fork.

4. Transfer to a heated platter and serve.

CURRIED RICE

Masala Bhat

This dish is the specialty of the Tamil Christians of South India. It is similar to the pilafs of North India but much simpler. I frequently make this rice dish to accompany simple sautéed or grilled chicken or seafood such as Pan-Grilled Scallops with Ajowan (page 96).

SERVES 4

$^1/_4$ cup finely chopped onion

1 teaspoon minced garlic

1 tablespoon vegetable oil

1 cup converted rice

$1^1/_2$ teaspoons Curry Powder (page 6)

2 cups Chicken Stock (page 25) or water

2 tablespoons finely chopped cilantro leaves

1 teaspoon coarse salt

1. Heat a heavy saucepan over medium-high heat. Add the onion, garlic, and oil and cook until the onion looks soft, about 2 minutes. Mix in the rice, Curry Powder, stock, cilantro, and salt. Bring to a boil. Decrease the heat to medium and cook, covered, for 20 minutes, or until the rice is cooked and the liquid is absorbed. Fluff the rice with a fork

2. Transfer to a heated platter and serve.

MINT RICE

Podina Chawal

A Persian and Moghul classic, this pilaf has many interpretations throughout India. This version is from the Himachal community at the extreme north, in the foothills of the Himalayas. Serve it with a curry such as Lamb Curry (page 118) or Chicken Curry (page 104).

SERVES 4

¹/4 cup finely chopped shallot

2 tablespoons minced mint

1 tablespoon vegetable oil

1 cup converted rice

2 cups Chicken Stock (page 25) or water

1 teaspoon coarse salt

2 tablespoons toasted pine nuts, for garnish

1. Heat a heavy saucepan over medium-high heat. Add the shallot, mint, and oil. Cook until the shallot is lightly fried, about 3 minutes. Add the rice, stock, and salt and bring to a boil. Decrease the heat to medium and cook, covered, for 20 minutes, or until the rice is cooked and the liquid is absorbed. Fluff the rice with a fork.

2. Transfer to a heated platter. Garnish with the pine nuts and serve.

SAFFRON PILAF

Zaffran Pulao

Delicately flavored with saffron and clove and embellished with raisins and nuts, this pilaf is perfect with the royal dishes of the Moghul.

SERVES 6

1/2 teaspoon saffron threads

1 cup basmati or regular long-grain rice

1 tablespoon *usli ghee* (page 185) or vegetable oil

1/2 cup chopped onion

2 tablespoons dark raisins

3 whole cloves

13/4 cups Chicken Stock (page 25)

Coarse salt

2 tablespoons toasted sliced almonds

1. Crumble 1/4 teaspoon of the saffron threads with your fingertips and put in a small bowl. Add the remaining saffron and 1 tablespoon warm water and set aside to soak. Rinse the rice thoroughly with cold water and put it in a large bowl. Add 2 cups cold water and soak for at least 30 minutes or up to 2 hours. Drain.

2. Heat the *usli ghee* in a saucepan over medium-high heat. Add the onion, raisins, and cloves. Cook, stirring constantly, until the onions look glazed, about 5 minutes. Add the stock, saffron solution, rice, and salt to taste. Bring to a boil.

3. Decrease the heat to medium and cook the rice, partially covered, for 8 minutes for basmati rice (13 minutes for regular rice) or until most of the liquid is absorbed and the surface of the rice is covered with steam holes. Cover the pan tightly and decrease the heat to as low as possible. Let the rice steam for 10 minutes. Remove from the heat and let the rice rest, covered and undisturbed, for 5 minutes. Fluff the rice with a fork.

4. Transfer to a heated platter, sprinkle the almonds on top, and serve.

SEMOLINA PILAF

Opama

In this popular pilaf from South India, the heat can range from very mild to fiery hot! I use very mild chiles, such as Anaheim, to keep the heat level low so that the subtle flavor of the semolina is not masked. For more flavor, add 12 kari leaves with the shallots. Opama is best with spicy dishes such as Cornish Hen Vindaloo (page 112) or Malabar Coconut Shrimp (page 98).

SERVES 6

$^1/_4$ cup vegetable oil

1 cup semolina or Cream of Wheat

$1^1/_2$ teaspoons mustard seeds

$^3/_4$ cup chopped shallots

1 tablespoon chopped green chiles

1 tablespoon chopped fresh ginger

$^1/_2$ cup frozen green peas

1 cup yogurt

$1^1/_4$ cups water

Coarse salt

$^1/_4$ cup chopped roasted cashews

1. Heat 2 tablespoons of the oil in a large heavy sauté pan over medium-high heat. Add the semolina and fry until the grains are evenly coated with the oil and lightly colored, about 6 minutes. Transfer to a bowl and wipe the pan clean with a paper towel.

2. Pour the remaining 2 tablespoons oil into the pan. When hot, add the mustard seeds and cover the pan with the lid because the seeds will pop and spatter. When the spluttering subsides, add the shallots, chiles, ginger, and peas and mix well. Whisk together the yogurt and water and add to the pan. Add the semolina and salt to taste. Cook, stirring gently, until the mixture thickens, about 5 minutes.

3. Decrease the heat to medium, cover, and cook for 5 minutes, or until most of the liquid is absorbed and the pilaf looks like dry polenta. Remove from the heat and let the pilaf rest, covered, for 10 minutes to become drier and fluffier. Fluff the pilaf with a fork. Transfer to a heated serving platter, sprinkle with the cashews, and serve.

MUNG BEAN PILAF

Pongal

This is a nutritious and filling pilaf with the distinct aroma of black pepper. For best results, use the special Tellicherry peppercorns.

SERVES 4

¹/₂ cup basmati rice

¹/₂ cup yellow mung beans

2 cups water

¹/₂ teaspoon roasted or plain cumin seeds

¹/₄ teaspoon turmeric

12 kari leaves, finely julienned

1¹/₂ teaspoons coarse salt

2 tablespoon *usli ghee* (page 185) or unsalted butter

1 teaspoon finely chopped fresh ginger

Freshly ground black pepper

1. Combine the rice and mung beans. Rinse well and place in a saucepan. Add the water, cumin, turmeric, kari leaves, salt, and 1 teaspoon of the *usli ghee*. Bring to a boil over medium-high heat. Stir occasionally to prevent lumping.

2. Decrease the heat to medium-low and gently boil for 15 minutes, or until most of the water is absorbed and the surface is covered with steam holes. Decrease the heat to as low as possible and cover the pot tightly. Steam until the rice and beans are soft but still hold their shape, about 10 minutes. Gently fold in the ginger and the remaining 1²/₃ tablespoons *usli ghee*. Transfer to a heated platter and serve sprinkled with black pepper.

Variation

Substitute red lentils for the mung beans. Replace the kari leaves with 2 tablespoons chopped dill.

LENTIL CREPES WITH GINGER AND ONION

Parupu Dosa

This is a lovely lentil and herb crepe created by my sister Roopa. It is a variation on the theme of the legume griddlecakes of South India. These crepes are quick and easy to make, and taste wonderful by themselves.

SERVES 4
MAKES 8 DOSAS

^{1}/$_2$ cup pink lentils

^{1}/$_2$ cup yellow mung beans

1 tablespoon yellow split peas

1 cup long-grain rice, preferably basmati

^{3}/$_4$ cup water, or as necessary

1 teaspoon coarse salt

1 tablespoon chopped fresh ginger

1 cup finely chopped onion

4 green chiles, stemmed and thinly sliced with seeds

^{3}/$_4$ cup chopped cilantro

Canola or vegetable oil, for cooking

1. Combine the lentils, mung beans, split peas, and rice. Rinse and place in a bowl. Add 4 cups of water and soak for 2 hours. Drain and place in the workbowl of a food processor. Grind until finely puréed, adding the water to form a mixture similar to lightly textured pancake batter. Transfer to a bowl and stir in the salt, ginger, onion, chiles, and cilantro.

2. Heat a nonstick griddle over high heat until very hot. Decrease the heat to medium-high and brush the griddle with oil. Add about ^{1}/$_3$ cup of the batter and spread into a 6-inch circle, about ^{1}/$_8$ inch thick. Pour 1 to 2 teaspoons oil around the crepe. Cook until the underside is browned, about 2 minutes, then flip the crepe. Cook the second side for 2 minutes, or until browned. Remove the crepe and keep warm while you repeat with the remaining batter. Transfer the crepes to heated plates and serve.

TANDOORI GRILLING

INDIAN baking, roasting, and grilling are done in a *tandoor,* a clay oven that is thought to have originated in Syria but today is used throughout central Asia. The Indians initially used the oven to bake bread, and this is still its main use. The breads, called *nan* (page 35), are slapped onto the sides of the *tandoor* where they stick on, puff up, and bake. Any meat, poultry, fish, or vegetable that can be threaded on skewers can also be cooked in a *tandoor.* The skewers are lowered into the *tandoor* pit and cooked. The meat remains tender and moist because it has been marinated in yogurt flavored with herbs and spices. Instructions in this chapter are for cooking *tandoor*-style dishes in a conventional oven or on a grill. I have created special marinades to replace the unique flavor of the *tandoor.*

TANDOORI CHICKEN

Tandoori Murgh

For Tandoori Chicken, the meat is marinated in yogurt spiced with ginger, garlic, and other fragrant spices and then cooked in a tandoor, *where it roasts and grills simultaneously. In order for the marinade to permeate the meat, the chicken is skinned and the meat pricked and slashed.*

SERVES 4

2 (2¹/4-pound) small chickens, split or quartered

2 tablespoons lemon juice

2 tablespoons yellow food coloring (optional)

1 tablespoon red food coloring (optional)

2 tablespoons ground cumin

1 tablespoon *Garam Masala* (page 7) or ground coriander

1 to 2 teaspoons ground red pepper

Coarse salt

2 cups yogurt

2 tablespoons grated fresh ginger

1 tablespoon minced garlic

6 tablespoons *usli ghee* (page 185), clarified butter, or extra-virgin olive oil

Onion, tomato, and cucumber slices, for garnish

1. Pull the skin off the chicken pieces, remove all visible fat, and discard. Prick the chicken all over with a fork and make diagonal slashes, ¹/2 inch deep and 1 inch apart, on the meat. Place in a large ceramic or glass bowl. Mix together the lemon juice, food colorings, cumin, *Garam Masala*, red pepper, and salt to taste and brush over the chicken, pushing the marinade into the slits. Combine the yogurt, ginger, and garlic and pour over the chicken. Mix, turning several times, to coat the chicken pieces evenly with the marinade. Cover and marinate at room temperature for 1 hour, or refrigerate for 8 hours or up to 2 days.

2. If the chicken has been refrigerated, bring to room temperature before cooking. If grilling, heat the grill and place the grill rack at least 5 inches from the heat. If roasting, place the oven rack in the middle position and preheat the oven to 500°.

3. Remove the chicken from the marinade and coat generously with *usli ghee*. To grill, place the chicken, meat side down, on the grill rack. To roast, place the chicken, meat side down, on a wire rack set over a jelly-roll pan. Grill or roast the chicken, turning 3 or 4 times during cooking, until the juices run clear, about 35 minutes. Brush the chicken with the remaining *usli ghee* and transfer to a platter.

4. Surround the chicken with slices of onion, tomato, and cucumber and serve.

NOTE: The tandoori marinade is traditionally colored bright orange using natural food coloring. This is purely for visual effect. You can omit the color if you prefer.

CHICKEN GINGER KEBABS

Murgh Tikka

Chicken kebabs are similar to Tandoori Chicken except that boneless chicken meat is used. Cut into bite-size pieces, the kebabs can be served as finger-food at a cocktail reception; pass them with Mint Chutney (page 159). For a more elaborate meal, serve them with Peach and Walnut Basmati Pilaf (page 59) or Baked Tandoori Bread (page 35) and Indian Salsa (page 164).

SERVES 4

2 pounds skinless and boneless chicken meat, cut into 1¹/₂ inch pieces

1 tablespoon ground coriander

Coarse salt

MARINADE

1 cup sour cream

4 tablespoons olive oil, for basting

3 tablespoons white wine vinegar

2 tablespoons grated fresh ginger

GARNISH

1 teaspoon minced garlic

Green and red bell pepper slices

1 tablespoon finely chopped green chiles

Thinly sliced scallions, white and green parts

¹/₂ teaspoon crushed ajowan seeds, or 1 teaspoon thyme

Cilantro leaves and tender stems

Lemon wedges

1. Put the chicken pieces in a large ceramic or glass bowl. Blend together all the marinade ingredients, including salt to taste, in another bowl. Pour the marinade over the chicken. Stir well to coat all the chicken pieces thoroughly. Cover and marinate at room temperature for 1 hour, or refrigerate for 4 hours or up to 1 day.

2. If the chicken has been refrigerated, bring to room temperature before cooking. If grilling, heat the grill and place the grill rack at least 5 inches from the heat. If roasting, preheat the oven to 500°.

3. Thread the chicken pieces on skewers. To grill, brush the skewers with oil and grill, turning often, until fully cooked, about 7 minutes. To roast, brush the skewers with oil and place in a single layer on a wire rack set over a jelly-roll pan. Roast, turning and basting with oil until the kebabs are fully cooked, about 10 minutes. Do not overcook, as they dry out easily.

4. Slide the kebabs off the skewers and arrange them on a heated platter. Surround them with pepper slices, scallions, cilantro, and lemon wedges, and serve.

NOTE: Although both light and dark chicken meat are used in this recipe, Indian cooks generally prefer the dark because it is more flavorful and stays moist.

TANDOORI FISH

Tandoori Machi

Tandoori Fish is the specialty of the Bengali Catholics of Portuguese descent. Although not as well known as Goan Portuguese food, Bengali Portuguese food, particularly certain fish preparations, is distinct and noteworthy. In this dish, fish kebabs, delicately flavored with a special tandoori marinade, are cooked to perfection. Serve the kebabs with any rice dish and Green Beans in Fenugreek Oil (page 132).

SERVES 4

MARINADE

1 teaspoon minced garlic

2 teaspoons grated fresh ginger

2 tablespoons heavy cream

1 tablespoon yellow food coloring (optional)

1/2 teaspoon ajowan seeds, crushed, or 1 teaspoon thyme

1/2 teaspoon freshly ground black pepper

Coarse salt

1 1/2 pounds skinless and boneless firm white fish, such as sea bass, turbot, or monkfish, cut into 1 1/2-inch cubes

2 onions, cut into 1-inch pieces

2 green peppers, cored and cut into 1-inch pieces

2 tablespoons melted butter, for basting

GARNISH

3 lemons, sliced

3 tomatoes, sliced

2 tablespoons chopped cilantro leaves

1. Put the fish pieces in a large ceramic or glass bowl. Add all the marinade ingredients, including, salt to taste, and toss well. Cover and marinate the fish for 30 minutes or refrigerate for 4 hours or up to 8 hours.

2. Preheat the grill or broiler. Place the grill rack 5 inches from the heat.

3. Thread the fish pieces on skewers alternating with pieces of onion and pepper. Brush generously with butter and place them in a single layer on the grill or under the broiler. Grill or broil, turning once and basting, until the fish is barely opaque, 5 to 6 minutes. Transfer the fish to a heated platter. Garnish with the lemon and tomato slices and chopped cilantro and serve.

TANDOORI SHRIMP

Tandoori Jheenga

These grilled shrimp are great for large-scale entertaining. Besides being attractive and delicious, they are very quick to make. For a light meal, serve a salad with them. For a more elaborate meal, include a pilaf, such as Saffron Pilaf (page 64), and Cauliflower with Nigella in Ginger Oil (page 135).

SERVES 4

1¹/₂ pounds large shrimp, peeled and deveined with tails left on

MARINADE

3 tablespoons yogurt

2 teaspoons grated fresh or prepared horseradish

1 tablespoon yellow food coloring (optional)

1 tablespoon minced garlic

1 tablespoon grated fresh ginger

2 teaspoons dry mustard

¹/₂ teaspoon ground red pepper

Coarse salt

2 onions, peeled and cut into 1-inch pieces

2 red bell peppers, cored and cut into 1-inch pieces

2 tablespoons melted butter, for basting

GARNISH

Tomato, cucumber, and lemon slices

1. Put the shrimp in a large ceramic or glass bowl. Add all of the marinade ingredients, including salt to taste, and toss well. Cover and marinate the shrimp for at least 10 minutes or up to 30 minutes.

2. Preheat the grill or broiler. Place the grill rack 5 inches from the heat.

3. Thread the shrimp on skewers, alternating with pieces of onion and pepper. Brush generously with butter and place them in a single layer on the grill or under the broiler. Grill or broil, turning often and basting, until the shrimp curl and turn pink, 6 to 7 minutes.

4. Transfer the skewers to a heated platter. Garnish with the tomato, cucumber, and lemon slices and serve.

Moghul Beef Kebabs

Pasanda Kabab

Pasanda *means "delicious pieces" and that is what these succulent morsels of spicy beef are. Yet another Moghul classic, they are the specialty of Pakistan, the country with which India shares the rich Moghul heritage. These kebabs are similar to Moghul Lamb Kebabs (page 79) except that here the marinade is accented with cardamom. A simple green salad and plain cooked rice will complete the meal.*

SERVES 4

1¹/₂ pounds beef sirloin, trimmed of excess fat, and cut into 1¹/₂-inch cubes

MARINADE

1 cup plain yogurt

¹/₄ cup lemon juice

2 teaspoons minced garlic

2 teaspoons grated fresh ginger

2 teaspoons ground cumin

2 teaspoons dry mustard

2 teaspoons dry mustard

1 teaspoon ground cardamom

3 tablespoons melted butter or extra virgin olive oil, for basting

Coarse salt and black pepper

GARNISH

1 small head lettuce, cored and shredded

12 red radishes

1. Pound the beef pieces, one at a time, to flatten them slightly. Set aside.

2. Combine all the marinade ingredients in a large bowl. Add the beef and mix, turning the meat several times to coat well with the marinade. Cover and marinate at room temperature for 1 hour, or refrigerate overnight or for up to 2 days.

3. If the beef has been refrigerated, bring to room temperature before cooking. If grilling, preheat the grill and place the grill rack at least 5 inches from the heat. If roasting, preheat the oven to 475°.

4. Lift the meat from the marinade and thread on skewers. Brush liberally with melted butter. To grill, place the skewers on the grill rack and cook,

turning and basting frequently, until cooked, about 10 minutes. To roast, arrange the skewers in a single layer on a wire rack set over a jelly-roll pan. Roast, turning and basting frequently, until cooked, about 8 minutes. The meat should be crusty on the outside and still pink in the middle.

5. To serve, slide the kebabs off the skewers onto a heated platter and sprinkle with salt and pepper. Surround the kebabs with lettuce and radishes. Serve immediately.

INDIAN-STYLE HAMBURGERS

Chapli Kabab

These kebabs, though shaped and cooked like American hamburgers, are, in fact, a Moghul classic. They can be made with ground lamb, beef, veal, chicken, or pork. Serve them in Indian bread, hamburger rolls, or pita pockets, if you like, topped with lettuce, onion, and tomato slices. The patties may be fried or grilled.

SERVES 4

1 pound ground lamb or beef

1 tablespoon *usli ghee* (page 185) or unsalted butter, melted

1 tablespoon thinly sliced green chiles

1/2 lightly packed cup chopped cilantro leaves and tender stems

1 cup finely chopped onion

1 teaspoon *Garam Masala* (page 7)

1/2 teaspoon black pepper

Coarse salt

Usli ghee (page 185), for brushing the grill

1. Combine all the ingredients thoroughly and shape into 4 hamburger patties.

2. To fry, heat a well-seasoned heavy griddle over medium-high heat. Add the patties. Cook, turning once, to the desired doneness, about 2 minutes on each side for rare, 3 minutes for medium, and 4 minutes for well done. To grill the hamburgers, heat the grill, arrange the grill rack 2 inches away from the heat, and brush lightly with *usli ghee*. Place the meat on the rack and grill, turning once, until done. The timing is the same as for frying.

MOGHUL LAMB KEBABS

Boti Kabab

Similar to shish kebab, these lamb kebabs are marinated in spiced yogurt flavored with plenty of cumin and black pepper and grilled to a melting tenderness. For a more complex flavoring, add 1 tablespoon Garam Masala *(page 7) to the marinade. Beef, pork, venison, and—a recent craze—buffalo all work well in this recipe. All the rice pilafs and breads in this book go well with these kebabs.*

SERVES 4

1¹/2 pounds lean boneless leg of lamb, trimmed of excess fat, and cut into 1¹/2-inch cubes

1 teaspoon ground red pepper

Coarse salt

MARINADE

1 cup plain yogurt

1/4 cup red wine vinegar

1 tablespoon minced garlic

2 teaspoons grated fresh ginger

2 tablespoons ground cumin

2 to 3 teaspoons cracked black peppercorns, preferably Tellicherry

3 tablespoons *usli ghee* (page 185), clarified butter, or vegetable oil, for basting

GARNISH

1/2 head lettuce, chopped

Green pepper slices

Carrot slices

1. Pound the lamb pieces, one at a time, to flatten them slightly. Set aside.

2. Combine all the marinade ingredients, including salt to taste, in a large bowl. Add the lamb and mix, turning the meat several times to coat well with the marinade. Cover and marinate at room temperature for 1 hour, or refrigerate overnight or for up to 2 days.

3. If the lamb has been refrigerated, bring to room temperatue before cooking. If grilling, preheat the grill and place the grill rack at least 5 inches from the heat. If roasting, preheat the oven to 475°. Lift the meat from the marinade and thread on skewers. Brush liberally with *usli ghee.*

(continued)

4. To grill, place the skewers on the grill rack and cook, turning and basting frequently, until cooked, about 10 minutes. To roast, arrange the skewers in a single layer on a wire rack set over a jelly-roll pan. Roast, turning and basting, until cooked, about 8 minutes. The meat should be crusty on the outside and still pink in the middle.

5. To serve, slide the kebabs off the skewers onto a heated platter and garnish with the lettuce, pepper, and carrot.

SPICE-RUBBED GRILLED LAMB

Bhona Gosht

An Anglo-Indian specialty, Bhona Gosht *is a true Raj period classic. It is popular in many of the exclusive Raj-style clubs in India, where the dish is still called Roast Mutton. A leg of lamb is boned and butterflied for ease of serving, then rubbed with seasonings. The meat can be left flat and grilled, or rolled and tied and roasted. Sweet fruit chutneys and Mint Rice (page 63) make ideal accompaniments. Any leftover meat can be sliced and served plain in a sandwich or stir-fried with vegetables, as in Country Captain (page 108) or Beef Frazer (page 129).*

SERVES 8

4 pounds boneless leg of lamb

SPICE RUB

1 tablespoon cumin seeds, crushed

1 tablespoon mustard seeds, crushed

1 tablespoon cracked black peppercorns

2 tablespoons paprika

2 tablespoons minced mint

2 tablespoons finely chopped garlic

$^1/_3$ cup white wine or lemon juice

$^1/_4$ cup *usli ghee* (page 185) or clarified butter, for basting

Coarse salt and black pepper

GARNISH

1 pound red, black, or white grapes

Mint sprigs

1. Score the thickest parts of the meat and pound to an even thickness. Prick the meat all over with a fork. Transfer to a shallow roasting pan. Combine all the spice rub ingredients and rub over the meat. Cover and marinate at room temperature for 2 hours, or refrigerate overnight or for up to 3 days.

2. Heat the grill and arrange the grill rack 5 inches from the heat.

3. Brush the meat liberally with 2 tablespoons of the *usli ghee*. Place the meat on the rack and grill, turning once and basting, until cooked according to taste: about 8 minutes per side for medium rare, 9 minutes

(continued)

for medium, and 10 minutes for well done. Let the meat rest on a carving board for 5 minutes before slicing.

4. Sprinkle the meat with salt and pepper, slice across the grain into thin slices, and arrange on a warm platter. Brush with the remaining *usli ghee* and surround with small bunches of grapes and mint sprigs. Serve immediately.

TANDOORI VEGETABLES

Tandoori Sabzi

To satisfy the vegetarian's desire for a tandoori-style dish, vegetables are coated with a yogurt marinade and grilled. The food coloring, though traditional, may be omitted if desired; the flavor will be the same. Serve the skewers with Tandoori Bread Stuffed with Cherries and Pistachios (page 47).

SERVES 4

8 cups vegetables cut into 2-inch pieces (see Note)

MARINADE

2 cups yogurt

¹/₄ cup red wine vinegar

6 tablespoons vegetable oil

3 tablespoons grated fresh ginger

1 tablespoon minced garlic

2 tablespoons yellow food coloring (optional)

1 tablespoon red food coloring (optional)

3 tablespoons ground cumin

1 tablespoon *Garam Masala* (page 7)

1 to 2 teaspoons ground red pepper

Coarse salt

¹/₃ cup *usli ghee* (page 185), clarified butter, or vegetable oil, for basting

GARNISH

Lemon slices and cilantro sprigs

1. Put the vegetables in a large bowl. Combine all the marinade ingredients, including salt to taste, and pour over the vegetables. Toss well to coat each piece with the marinade. Cover and marinate at room temperature for 4 hours or refrigerate for up to 2 days.

2. If the vegetables have been refrigerated, bring to room temperature before cooking. If grilling, heat the grill and place the grill rack at least 3 inches from the heat. If roasting, place the oven rack in the middle position and preheat the oven to 500°.

(continued)

3. Remove the vegetables from the marinade and thread them on skewers. Coat generously with 3 tablespoons *usli ghee*, place on the rack, and grill, turning and basting several times, until cooked and browned, about 25 minutes. Brush the vegetables with the remaining *usli ghee* and transfer to a platter.

4. Surround the vegetables with lemon slices and cilantro sprigs and serve.

NOTE: Use a combination of at least 4 vegetables, such as cauliflower, red bell pepper, green bell pepper, turnip, mushrooms, zucchini, yellow squash, pattypan squash, brussels sprouts, endive, radish, eggplant, onion, shallots, and/or scallions.

TANDOORI QUAIL
with Tamarind-Pepper Glaze

Tandoori Titar

Tandoori-grilled smoky quails and similar game birds are the specialties of north-western India and Pakistan, where grain fields and fruit orchards abound. Mint Rice (page 63) makes a lovely accompaniment.

SERVES 4

8 quails

MARINADE

3 tablespoons clarified butter, melted, or vegetable oil

1/4 cup tamarind juice

2 tablespoons lemon juice

2 teaspoons minced garlic

1 tablespoon grated fresh ginger

1 teaspoon ground cardamom

1/2 teaspoon cayenne pepper

1 1/2 teaspoons coarsely ground black pepper

1 1/2 teaspoons coarse salt

1. Split quails lengthwise and place on a work surface, breast side up. Press down to break the breastbone and flatten. Place in a shallow dish.

2. Combine the marinade ingredients and pour over the quails. Turn and toss to coat thoroughly. Cover and marinate for 15 minutes at room temperature, or 4 hours to overnight in the refrigerator. Remove from the refrigerator at least 15 minutes before cooking. If grilling, heat the grill and place the grill rack at least 5 inches from the heat. If roasting, preheat the oven to 500° and place a rack in the middle position.

3. To grill, remove quails from the marinade and place meat side down on the grill rack. To roast, remove quails from the marinade and place meat side down on a wire rack set over a jelly-roll pan. Grill or roast the quails, turning once and basting with pan juices, for 15 minutes, or until medium rare (meat will be pink near the bones). If desired, brush the quails with more butter before serving.

FISH
AND SHELLFISH

Surrounded on three sides by ocean, India has a rich tradition of cooking fish and shellfish. Tuna, sea bass, trout, sole, salmon, and kingfish are common everyday fare, while lobsters, shrimps, giant prawns, tiny mussels, and squid are treated with great creativity. The four distinct communities excelling in this art are the Bengalis in the east, the Tamils in the south, and the Malabaris and Goans to the southwest. Bengalis are famous for their mustard-laced fish, the Tamils for their tamarind-flavored fish, and the Malabaris and Goans for their use of coconut and chiles. The recipes chosen for this book are made with the most readily available fish and shellfish in the market, which adapt perfectly to Indian cooking. Remember your dish is going to be only as good as the ingredients, so buy only the freshest available. It is quite acceptable to use substitutes, and I have made recommendations to guide you.

Spring Smoked Salmon Kedgeree with Dill   88
Kedgeree

Steamed Fish in Herb Sauce   90
Patrani Machi

Bengal Fragrant Fish Curry   92
Maach Bhaja

Madras Hot Fish Curry with Tamarind   93
Meen Kari

Goan Warm Mussel Salad   95
Tisru

Pan-Grilled Scallops with Ajowan   96
Bhoni Machi

Moghul Shrimp in Cream Sauce   97
Malai Jheenga

Malabar Coconut Shrimp   98
Konjupa

Parsi Breaded Shrimp in Green Paste   99
Jheenga Patia

Lobster with Spice Butter   100
Bagda Jingri

Salmon Molee   101
Meen Molee

SMOKED SALMON KEDGEREE with Dill

Kedgeree

Kedgeree is the Anglicized pronunciation of the Indian kecheree, a popular North Indian rice and lentil dish that looks much like risotto. The English replaced the lentils with cooked or smoked fish, added herbs and cream sauce, and turned peasant fare into an elegant brunchtime delicacy. Kedgeree is very popular with Anglo-Indians, who make it with locally available seafood, including smoked trout, sardines, sole, sea bass, Bombay duck (a type of flying fish), shrimp, mussels, and scallops. While salmon is not an Indian fish, I think it works well here, both in taste and visual appeal. You can use any smoked fish in place of the salmon.

SERVES 4

4 ounces smoked salmon, cut into bite-size pieces

$^1/_2$ teaspoon coarsely ground black pepper

2 tablespoons chopped dill

3 tablespoons unsalted butter

1 teaspoon coarse salt

1 cup converted rice

$^1/_4$ cup finely diced onion

1 tablespoon all-purpose flour

$1^1/_4$ cups milk

6 hard-boiled eggs, peeled and cut into wedges (optional)

1 lemon, cut into wedges (optional)

2 tablespoons chopped parsley

Dill sprigs, for garnish

1. Toss the salmon with the pepper and 1 tablespoon of the dill and set aside.

2. Combine 2 cups water, 1 tablespoon of the butter, and salt in a medium saucepan. Bring to a boil over high heat. Stir in the rice, decrease the heat to medium-low, and simmer, covered, for 20 minutes, or until the water is absorbed and the rice is tender.

3. Melt the remaining 2 tablespoons butter in a large frying pan over medium-high heat. Add the onion and cook until soft, about 3 minutes. Add the flour and cook, stirring, until it is fried but not browned, about

2 minutes. Add the milk and the remaining 1 tablespoon dill and cook, stirring constantly, for 2 minutes or until the sauce thickens. Decrease the heat, fold in the rice, and cook until heated through. Transfer to a heated serving platter.

4. Arrange the salmon on top of the rice and surround with the egg and lemon wedges. Sprinkle with parsley, garnish with dill, and serve.

STEAMED FISH
in Herb Sauce

Patrani Machi

Bombay's Parsi community excels in fish cookery, and Patrani Machi *is their sig-nature dish. (The Parsis are a sect that was driven out of Persia in the ninth cen-tury and settled in India's western coastal region.) Traditionally, this dish is made with hilsa, a local fish known for both its rich flavor and its innumerable bones, and is steamed in banana leaves. I have found that salmon fillets make a flavor-ful, appealing, and convenient substitute. I also prefer to use edible wrappers, such as lettuce (you can also use spinach, swiss chard, cabbage, and taro leaves). This dish is traditionally served with steamed rice, but is also good with a light pilaf, such as Lemon Pilaf (page 58). It can be made ahead and served straight from the refrigerator as a first course.*

SERVES 4

1¹/₂ pounds boneless, skinless
   salmon fillets

HERB SAUCE

¹/₃ cup sweetened shredded coconut

3 garlic cloves, peeled

1 to 4 green chiles, stemmed (depend-ing on desired level of heat)

3 tablespoons lemon juice

¹/₂ firmly packed cup cilantro leaves
   and tender stems

¹/₄ firmly packed cup mint leaves

Coarse salt

8 large lettuce leaves, blanched and
   trimmed

GARNISH

2 tablespoons finely chopped
   toasted almonds

1 teaspoon toasted cumin seeds

1 tablespoon finely chopped
   fresh ginger

1 teaspoon finely minced lemon zest

1. Cut the fish into 4 serving portions and set aside.

2. Rinse the coconut under warm running water and drain. Combine the coconut, garlic, chiles, lemon juice, cilantro, and mint in the workbowl

of a food processor and process until minced. Transfer to a bowl. Stir in the salt to taste. Add the fish and toss well to coat.

3. Place 2 lettuce leaves on a work surface, overlapping them slightly. Place 1 piece of fish on top of the lettuce leaves, fold in the sides, and close up into a neat package. Prepare the remaining pieces the same way. Transfer the packages to a steamer rack or put 2 packages in each of 2 bamboo steamer trays. Steam until the fish is just cooked, about 6 minutes.

4. To serve, transfer the fish packets to warm dinner plates and open leaves. Garnish with the almonds, cumin seeds, ginger, and lemon zest.

Bengal Fragrant Fish Curry

Maach Bhaja

An everyday dish from Bengal in eastern India, this is a light fish dish with lots of spices in a tomato sauce. Plain rice is the best choice to serve with it.

Serves 4

4 cod, haddock, or tuna steaks

1 teaspoon dry mustard

1 teaspoon ground cumin

$^1/_2$ teaspoon turmeric

$^1/_2$ teaspoon ground red pepper

2 tablespoons mustard oil (page 182) or vegetable oil

1 cup thinly sliced onion

1 tablespoon sliced garlic

1 tablespoon shredded green chiles

2 cups chopped peeled tomatoes

Coarse salt

Juice of $^1/_2$ lemon

$^1/_4$ cup finely chopped cilantro leaves and tender stems

1. Place the fish steaks on a plate and sprinkle with mustard, cumin, turmeric, and red pepper. Rub the spices all over the fish and set aside. Heat 1 tablespoon of the oil in a large heavy nonstick sauté pan over high heat. If you are using the mustard oil, let it smoke for a moment to rid it of its pungency. Add the fish and sauté, turning once, until seared, about 1 minute. Transfer to a plate.

2. Decrease the heat to medium and add the remaining 1 tablespoon oil, the onion, garlic, and chiles. Cook, stirring occasionally, until the onion begins to brown, about 5 minutes. Add 1 cup of the tomatoes, along with the accumulated juices, and salt to taste. Continue to cook until the sauce thickens a little, about 5 minutes. Add the fish steaks and the remaining 1 cup tomatoes and cook until the sauce is bubbling and the fish is heated through, about 4 minutes. Transfer the fish and the sauce to a heated serving platter.

3. Sprinkle with lemon juice and cilantro and serve.

MADRAS HOT FISH CURRY
with Tamarind

Meen Kari

Try this dish even if you have never cooked with tamarind before. In this specialty from Tamil Nadu on the southern shores of India, the fish gets its piquant flavor from the tamarind and heat from red pepper. Traditionally Meen Kari is made very hot, but you can tone down the heat by reducing the amount of red pepper. Remember, however, to reduce the tamarind, too, or the dish will taste too sour. Serve with plain rice and Banana-Coconut Yogurt Salad (page 155).

SERVES 4

1¹/2 pounds skinless and boneless sole or flounder fillets, cut into 4 serving pieces

1 tablespoon Curry Powder (page 6)

1 tablespoon ground red pepper, paprika, or a combination

3 tablespoons vegetable oil

¹/4 cup all-purpose flour, for dusting

1 teaspoon mustard seeds

¹/2 cup finely chopped onion

1 teaspoon minced garlic

12 kari leaves, or 2 bay leaves

2 cups water

2 tablespoons tomato paste

1 teaspoon tamarind paste (page 184) or lemon juice

¹/2 cup coconut milk, light cream, or low-fat milk

Coarse salt

1. Place the fish on a plate. Combine the curry powder and red pepper and rub over the fish. Heat 2 tablespoons of the oil in a large heavy non-stick sauté pan over medium-high heat until hot. Lightly dust the fish with flour and add to the oil. Cook until the fish is lightly browned, about 1 minute. Do not fully cook the fish. Return the fish to the plate and set aside.

2. Wipe the pan clean and add the remaining 1 tablespoon oil over medium-high heat. When the oil is hot, add the mustard seeds and cover the pan with the lid because the seeds will pop and spatter. When the

(continued)

93

sputtering subsides, add the onion, garlic, and kari leaves. Cook until the onions are soft, about 3 minutes. Stir in the water, tomato paste, and tamarind paste and boil the sauce until reduced and thick, about 5 minutes. Add the coconut milk, salt to taste, and the fish. Cook until the sauce is piping hot and fish is heated through.

3. Serve warm, at room temperature, or cold, straight from the refrigerator.

GOAN WARM MUSSEL SALAD

Tisru

In this salad from Goa, once a Portuguese colony, coconut mellows the spices and harmonizes them with the mussels. Tisru is traditionally served with sweet buttery dinner rolls for mopping up the sauce. Plain rice or Indian bread would also pair well.

SERVES 4

2 tablespoons vegetable oil

1 cup finely chopped onion

1 tablespoon finely shredded
   fresh ginger

1 tablespoon ground coriander

1 teaspoon turmeric

$^1/_2$ to 1 teaspoon ground red pepper

$^1/_2$ cup coconut milk, fresh (page 179)
   or canned

Coarse salt

4 pounds mussels (about 4 dozen),
   scrubbed clean

Juice of 1 small lemon

2 tablespoons chopped cilantro leaves
   and tender stems

2 tablespoons grated unsweetened
   coconut (optional)

1. Place the oil and onion in a deep pot over high heat and cook, stirring, until the onion begins to brown, about 5 minutes. Lower the heat and stir in the ginger, coriander, turmeric, and red pepper. Cook for 1 minute. Stir in the coconut milk, salt to taste, and mussels and bring to a boil.

2. Steam, covered, until the mussels open, about 7 minutes. Discard any mussels that don't open. Transfer the mussels and the sauce to a deep platter.

3. Sprinkle with lemon juice, cilantro, and coconut. Serve immediately.

Variation —————————————————————————

Little neck or manila clams can be used in place of the mussels.

95

PAN-GRILLED SCALLOPS
with Ajowan

Bhoni Machi

This is one of the mildest, most delicate, and most elegant preparations from the coastal city of Bombay. Traditionally, pomfret, a white fish, is used, but scallops work beautifully. Serve the scallops with Green Pea Pilaf (page 61) and Curried Eggplant with Chutney (page 136).

SERVES 4

1^1/$_2$ pounds scallops, preferably bay

^{1}/$_4$ teaspoon ajowan seeds

^{1}/$_4$ teaspoon crushed red pepper flakes

1 teaspoon minced garlic

1 tablespoon lemon juice

2 tablespoons minced cilantro leaves and tender stems

1 tablespoon minced basil

1^1/$_2$ tablespoons vegetable oil

1. Put the scallops in a bowl. Combine the ajowan, red pepper, garlic, lemon juice, cilantro, basil, and oil and rub over the scallops.

2. Heat a large heavy nonstick sauté pan over high heat. When the pan is very hot, add the scallops and cook, shaking and tossing, until they turn ivory white and opaque, about 2 minutes for bay scallops, 3 minutes for sea scallops.

3. Serve immediately.

MOGHUL SHRIMP IN CREAM SAUCE

Malai Jheenga

Shrimp in cream sauce is a classic Moghul preparation. The unique flavor and creamy consistency of the dish come from coconut milk. Scallops, lobster, crab, conch, and fish can be used in place of shrimp. Saffron Pilaf (page 64) or Flame-Roasted Puffy Bread (page 34) would be good to serve with it.

SERVES 4

$^1/_4$ cup vegetable oil

1 cup finely chopped red onions

$^1/_2$ cup finely chopped shallots

2 bay leaves

$^1/_2$ teaspoon fennel seeds, crushed

4 whole cloves

2 teaspoons ground coriander

$^1/_4$ teaspoon turmeric

$^1/_4$ to $^1/_2$ teaspoon ground red pepper

1 pound medium shrimp, peeled and deveined

1 cup coconut milk, fresh (page 179) or canned, or light cream

Coarse salt

2 tablespoons heavy cream (optional)

1. Heat the oil in a medium saucepan over medium-high heat and add the onion, shallots, bay leaves, fennel, cloves, coriander, turmeric, and red pepper. Cook, stirring often, until the onion begins to brown, about 5 minutes. Add the shrimps and sauté until they begin to curl and turn pink, 2 to 3 minutes. Stir in the coconut milk and cook until the sauce is bubbling hot. Season with salt to taste and add the cream.

2. Serve immediately.

MALABAR COCONUT SHRIMP

Konjupa

This dish is from Malabar, the sultry coastal region along the southwestern shores of India. Konjupa are tiny shrimps found in the local waters. They are cooked in coconut sauce with fresh ginger, green chiles, and cumin. The Malabar people like their konjupa very hot but you can tone down the heat by reducing the number of chiles. Serve them with Semolina Pilaf (page 65) and Curry-Scented Mushrooms (page 140).

SERVES 4

3 tablespoons vegetable oil

1 teaspoon mustard seeds

1 teaspoon chopped garlic

1 cup finely chopped red onion

1 teaspoon cumin seeds, crushed

2 tablespoons shredded fresh ginger

2 to 8 green chiles, stemmed, seeded, and shredded

24 kari leaves, or 2 tablespoons chopped cilantro leaves and tender stems

2 cups coconut milk, fresh (page 179) or canned

$1^{1}/_{2}$ pounds medium shrimp, peeled and deveined

Coarse salt

1. Heat the oil in a large heavy nonstick sauté pan over medium-high heat. When the oil is hot, add the mustard seeds and cover the pan with the lid because the seeds will pop and spatter. When the sputtering subsides, add the garlic and onion. Cook, stirring occasionally, until the onions begin to color, about 6 minutes. Stir in the cumin, ginger, chiles to taste, kari leaves (if using), and coconut milk and bring to a boil. Cook, uncovered, until the sauce thickens, about 8 minutes.

2. Add the shrimp and cook, stirring constantly, until they curl up and turn pink, about 3 minutes. Add salt to taste. If you are using cilantro, add it now.

3. Serve immediately.

PARSI BREADED SHRIMP
in Green Paste

Jheenga Patia

Parsis like their food very hot. In this dish, they would use chiles like habaneros, jalapeños, or Thai bird peppers. I personally like a moderate flavorful heat that dances on my palate. Accordingly, I would use a combination of chiles, mostly Anaheims with an arbol or two thrown in. Accompany the shrimp with a chutney such as Peach Chutney with Walnuts and Saffron (page 163).

SERVES 4

1¹/₂ pounds jumbo shrimp

GREEN PASTE

1 lightly packed cup cilantro leaves
   and tender stems

¹/₂ cup mint leaves

¹/₂ cup grated unsweetened coconut

¹/₄ cup lemon juice

5 cloves garlic, peeled

2 to 8 green chiles, stemmed

1 tablespoon sugar

Coarse salt

Vegetable oil, for shallow frying

2 large eggs, lightly beaten

3 cups dried bread crumbs

1. Peel, devein, and butterfly the shrimp, leaving the tails on. Rinse and pat dry on towels. Thread a toothpick along the length of each shrimp.

2. Combine all the ingredients, including salt to taste, for the green paste in a food processor or electric blender. Process into a paste and transfer to a bowl. Add the shrimp and toss to coat thoroughly.

3. Pour the oil to a depth of ¹/₂ inch into a large skillet and heat to 375° over medium-high heat. Dip the shrimp into the beaten eggs and then into bread crumbs. Slip them into the hot oil, in batches if necessary, and fry, turning, until cooked through and the coating is golden, about 3 minutes. Remove with a slotted spoon and drain on paper towels.

4. Arrange the shrimp on a platter and serve with a chutney.

LOBSTER
with Spice Butter

Bagda Jingri

Cooking fish or shellfish with Panch Phoron *is a popular technique throughout eastern India. Although it is not traditional, I like to add a little tomato paste to the sauce. In addition to lending a piquant undertone, it helps round out the flavor. You can use crab, scallops, mussels, clams, shrimp, kingfish, sea bass, or haddock in place of the lobster.*

SERVES 4

3/4 pound cooked lobster meat

8 small red new potatoes

1 pound eggplant, preferably small Italian or long Japanese eggplant

2 tablespoons mustard oil (page 182) or vegetable oil

1 1/2 teaspoons *Panch Phoron* (page 8)

1 teaspoon turmeric

2 cups water

Coarse salt

1 tablespoon tomato paste

1 to 4 green chiles, stemmed, seeded, and shredded

2 tablespoons chopped cilantro leaves and tender stems

1. Pick over the lobster meat to remove any shells and cut it into large pieces. Scrub the potatoes and peel partially. Prick all over with a fork. If using tiny Italian eggplants, leave them whole. Otherwise, cut the eggplant into 1 1/2-inch pieces.

2. Heat the oil in a large saucepan over medium-high heat. If you are using mustard oil, let it smoke for a moment to rid it of its pungency. When the oil is hot, add the *Panch Phoron*. When the spices have turned several shades darker, add the turmeric, potatoes, and eggplant and mix well. Fry the vegetables, turning until they are well coated with oil, about 6 minutes.

3. Add the water and salt to taste. Cover and cook over medium heat until the vegetables are tender, about 20 minutes. Stir in the tomato paste and chiles, and then fold in the lobster meat. Cook until heated through. Sprinkle with cilantro and serve.

SALMON MOLEE

Meen Molee

Coconut and fish play pivotal roles in the cooking of the southern coastal Indian states. Molee, a coconut braised preparation, can be made with any number of fish, such as tuna, halibut, and mackerel, as well as seafood, such as shrimp, scallops, and squid. Serve this simple, delicious preparation with plain cooked rice or any pilaf.

SERVES 4

1¹/₂ pounds salmon fillet, skin on

¹/₂ teaspoon turmeric, or 1 teaspoon Curry Powder (page 6)

¹/₂ teaspoon ground red pepper

Coarse salt

Juice of 1 lime

¹/₄ cup canola or vegetable oil

1 onion, peeled, halved, and thinly sliced

1 teaspoon cumin seeds, lightly crushed

¹/₂ teaspoon fennel seeds, lightly crushed

24 kari leaves, fresh or dried

2 teaspoons grated fresh ginger

2 to 4 green chiles, stemmed and thickly sliced lengthwise

1 cup coconut milk

1. Place the salmon on a plate. Combine the turmeric, red pepper, salt, and lime juice and rub over the salmon.

2. Heat 2 tablespoons of the oil in a large nonstick sauté pan over high heat until hot. Add the salmon fillets and cook, turning once, until lightly browned, about 1 minute. Do not fully cook. Return the fish to the plate.

3. Add the remaining 2 tablespoons oil, onion, cumin, and fennel to the pan. Cook over medium-high heat, stirring occasionally, until the onion is light golden, about 5 minutes. Stir in the kari leaves, ginger, and chiles and cook for 1 minute. Add the coconut milk and bring to a boil. Gently boil until reduced by half, about 5 minutes. Return the salmon, with its juices, to the pan and cook, basting with the sauce, until heated through, about 2 minutes. Transfer to a heated platter and serve immediately.

CHICKEN
AND POULTRY

Ask any Indian cook which meat is the most highly esteemed and he will tell you chicken because it is the most adaptable to Indian flavors. Among the best Indian chicken preparations are Tandoori Chicken and Chicken Biriyani. In the Indian way of cooking, the skin is always removed and discarded so that the spices can penetrate better into the meat. For best results, use small chickens or Cornish hens, preferably free range; they are more flavorful than big factory-farm birds.

In India, duck is treated as game, hence its use is restricted to only certain communities. The preparations have a festive tone and are reserved for special occasions. The recipe included in this book is just such a standout dish (see page 114).

CHICKEN CURRY

Murgh Masala

A Punjabi specialty from North India, this chicken curry is fragrant with cumin and cilantro. It is this distinctive aroma that is often associated with Indian food and that has captured the hearts and palates of people around the globe. This curry can also be made with other birds. Serve it with a rice dish or bread.

SERVES 4

1 (3-pound) chicken, cut into 8 to 10 pieces and skinned

1¹/₂ cups finely chopped onion

2 tablespoons grated or crushed fresh ginger

1 tablespoon minced garlic

1 tablespoon paprika

¹/₂ teaspoon ground red pepper

1¹/₂ pounds ripe tomatoes, puréed with skin

Coarse salt

1 cup water

2 teaspoons ground toasted cumin seeds or *Garam Masala* (page 7)

¹/₂ cup finely chopped cilantro leaves and tender stems

1. Heat a large heavy nonstick sauté pan over medium-high heat. Add the chicken pieces and sauté, turning until they lose their pink color and are seared, about 5 minutes. Add the onion, ginger, and garlic. Sauté, stirring, until the onion is lightly browned, about 8 minutes. It will brown unevenly, which is as it should be for the complex flavoring of the finished sauce. Add the paprika, red pepper, tomatoes, and salt to taste.

2. Pour the water over the chicken and bring to a boil. Decrease the heat and simmer, covered, until the chicken is very tender, about 30 minutes. If the sauce is too thin, increase the heat and boil rapidly, uncovered, until it reduces to the desired consistency (like a pasta sauce). Stir in the cumin and half of the cilantro and transfer to a warm serving dish.

3. Sprinkle with the remaining cilantro and serve.

CHICKEN IN CREAM SAUCE

Makhani Murgh

Also known as butter chicken, this dish is made by braising pieces of day-old grilled chicken, preferably tandoori style, in a creamy tomato sauce. Green Pea Pilaf (page 61) or Baked Tandoori Bread (page 35) both make excellent accompaniments.

SERVES 4

4 tablespoons unsalted butter

1 recipe Tandoori Chicken (page 70), or 2 small roasted chickens, cut into serving pieces and skinned

2 teaspoons ground cumin

SAUCE

2 cups tomato purée

1 cup heavy cream

$1/4$ cup julienned fresh ginger

$1/2$ cup finely chopped cilantro leaves and tender stems

Coarse salt and black pepper

1. Melt 2 tablespoons of the butter in a large heavy nonstick sauté pan over medium-high heat. Add the chicken pieces, sprinkle with the cumin, and sauté, turning, for 3 minutes. Add the sauce ingredients and simmer until the chicken absorbs some of the sauce and becomes meltingly tender, 15 minutes. Stir in the remaining 2 tablespoons butter. *(The dish may be made ahead and refrigerated for up to 2 days. Reheat it and check the seasonings, adding more pepper and chopped cilantro, if necessary.)*

2. Transfer to a warm dish and serve.

NOTE: For a hotter-tasting dish, fold in up to 4 green chiles, stemmed and minced with seeds, into the sauce.

CHICKEN BIRIYANI

Murgh Biriyani

A biriyani is a Moghul rice casserole similar to a pilaf, in which a korma, a rich and aromatic braised preparation, is layered with basmati rice and baked. Biriyanis are festive dishes usually served on special occasions in India. Since the preparation is rather simple, try serving a biriyani at a dinner party. An interesting touch I have added to this biriyani is mango chutney, which makes the casserole intriguingly spicy. Biriyani is a very satisfying one-dish meal. All you need to complete the meal is a green salad.

SERVES 4

1 recipe Moghul Chicken Korma (page 107)

¹/₄ cup Chicken Stock (page 25), milk, or water

2 tablespoons Sweet Mango Chutney (page 162), or storebought, finely chopped

2¹/₂ cups cooked rice

¹/₄ cup dark raisins

Coarse salt

2 tablespoons toasted sliced almonds, for garnish

1. Place the rack in the middle of the oven and preheat the oven to 350°.

2. Combine the chicken korma, stock, and chutney in an ovenproof dish. Carefully fold in the rice and raisins. Season with salt to taste and cover the dish. Place in the oven for 30 minutes, or until the *biriyani* is piping hot and the flavors have blended through. Transfer to a warm platter, garnish with the almonds, and serve.

Variation

Lamb, beef, shrimp, or vegetables all make excellent substitutes for the chicken in this *biriyani*.

MOGHUL CHICKEN KORMA

Murgh Korma

Korma is traditionally a mild creamy preparation but you can make it spicy by adding ground red pepper if you like. Serve it with Saffron Pilaf (page 64) or stuffed bread. A common use of korma *is in* biriyani, *the Moghul rice-and-meat casserole.*

SERVES 4

1 pound skinless and boneless chicken breast

1/4 cup vegetable oil

1 1/2 cups finely chopped onion

1 teaspoon minced garlic

2 teaspoons *Garam Masala* (page 7), or 1 tablespoon ground coriander

1 cup coconut milk

Coarse salt

1/4 cup coconut cream or coconut milk

2 tablespoons toasted sliced almonds

1. Cut the chicken into 1-inch-wide strips. Cut each strip into 1/2-inch pieces. Set aside.

2. Heat the oil in a large heavy nonstick sauté pan over medium-high heat. Add the onion and garlic. If you are using coriander, add it now. Cook until the onion begins to color, about 5 minutes. Add the chicken and continue to cook until it loses its pink color, about 4 minutes.

3. Stir in the coconut milk and salt to taste and bring the sauce to a boil. Decrease the heat and simmer, covered, until the chicken is tender and the sauce is reduced and thick, about 15 minutes. If the sauce is too thin, increase the heat and boil it, uncovered, until reduced to the desired consistency. Mix in the *Garam Masala* and coconut cream and heat thoroughly. Transfer to a warm dish.

4. Sprinkle with almonds and serve.

COUNTRY CAPTAIN

Kapitan

An Anglo-Indian specialty, Country Captain is essentially leftover meat warmed in a curry-and-vegetable sauce. It is an easy and quick technique that produces delicious results. You can also make this dish with leftover Roast Duck with Cinnamon-Plum Glaze (page 114), Tandoori Chicken (page 70), or any other roast poultry or meat.

SERVES 2

3/4 pound leftover cooked chicken or meat

3 tablespoons unsalted butter

1 teaspoon finely chopped garlic

2 teaspoons Curry Powder (page 6)

1 1/2 cups chopped onion

2 teaspoons all-purpose flour

1 teaspoon Worcestershire sauce

1/3 cup heavy cream or Chicken Stock (page 25)

1 green bell pepper, cored and julienned

1 red bell pepper, cored and julienned

1/2 cup of 1-inch cubes pineapple

Freshly ground black pepper

1/4 cup roasted cashews or slivered almonds (optional)

1. Cut the chicken into 1 1/2-inch pieces.

2. Heat the butter in a large heavy nonstick sauté pan over medium-high heat. Add the garlic, Curry Powder, and onion, and cook, stirring occasionally, for 2 minutes, or until the onion is barely soft. Add the flour and cook, stirring, for 1 minute. Stir in the Worcestershire sauce and cream and bring the sauce to a boil.

3. Add the green and red bell peppers. Decrease the heat to medium and cook, stirring and tossing, for 5 minutes, or until the vegetables are barely soft. Fold in the chicken and cook until heated through. Fold in the pineapple. Transfer to a serving platter.

4. Sprinkle with pepper, scatter the cashews on top, and serve immediately.

KARHAI CHICKEN
with Peppers and Tomatoes

Karhai Murgh Khasa

"Karhai" is the Indian wok, similar to the Chinese except heavier and deeper. In this preparation from the northwest province of India and Pakistan, the chicken is cooked with vegetables and spices. The initial braising and final pan-roasting gives the dish unique smoky sweetness. Serve with any bread or a rice dish.

SERVES 4

1 pound boneless, skinless chicken breast, cut into 1-inch cubes

1 teaspoon minced garlic

2 teaspoons grated fresh ginger

2 teaspoons ground coriander

$^1/_2$ to 1 teaspoon ground red pepper

$^1/_2$ teaspoon turmeric

1 teaspoon coarse salt

4 red ripe tomatoes

3 tablespoons canola or vegetable oil

1 onion, peeled and chopped into 1-inch pieces

1 red bell pepper, cored and cut into 1-inch pieces

1 green bell pepper, cored and cut into 1-inch pieces

$^1/_2$ teaspoon *Garam Masala* (page 7) or roasted cumin seeds

4 tablespoons chopped cilantro

Coarsely ground black pepper

1. Place the chicken in a bowl and toss with garlic, ginger, coriander, red pepper, turmeric, and salt. In a blender or food processor, purée 2 of the tomatoes, with the skin. Cut the other 2 tomatoes into 1-inch wedges.

2. Heat 2 tablespoons of the oil in a large *karhai* or skillet over high heat. Add the chicken and sear, turning, until browned, about 8 minutes. Add the tomato purée and cook, covered, over medium heat, until the chicken is tender and the sauce has reduced and thickened, about 15 minutes.

3. Add the onion, peppers, sliced tomatoes, and remaining 1 tablespoon oil. Stir-fry until the vegetables are cooked and chicken is lightly seared, about 6 minutes. Transfer to a heated platter, sprinkle with the *Garam Masala*, cilantro, and black pepper, and serve immediately.

ROYAL BRAISED CORNISH HENS

Shahi Korma

This exquisitely flavored korma *comes directly from the royal kitchens of the Moghul emperor Shahjahan, who built the beautiful Taj Mahal. The addition of ginger, garlic, paprika, and turmeric gives the gravy a rich, nutty flavor. Chicken makes a fine substitute for the Cornish hens, or for a special flavor, substitute the hens with squab, quail, or rabbit.*

SERVES 4

$1/4$ cup canola or olive oil

2 Cornish hens, skinned and quartered

$1^1/2$ cups finely chopped onion

1 tablespoon finely chopped fresh ginger

1 teaspoon finely chopped garlic

4 tablespoons ground blanched almonds

4 tablespoons freshly ground coriander seeds

1 tablespoon freshly ground green cardamom seeds

1 tablespoon paprika

1 teaspoon ground red pepper

$1/2$ teaspoon turmeric

1 cup plain low-fat yogurt, lightly beaten

$1^1/2$ teaspoons coarse salt

1. Heat 1 tablespoon of the oil in a sauté pan over medium-high heat. When the oil is hot, add the hens and cook until they lose their pink color and are lightly browned, about 3 minutes. Transfer to a bowl.

2. Add the remaining 3 tablespoons oil to the pan along with the onion and cook over medium-high heat until light brown, about 8 minutes. Add the ginger, garlic, almonds, coriander, cardamom, paprika, red pepper, and turmeric. Cook the spices, stirring, for 2 minutes. Fold in the yogurt, $1/3$ cup at a time, stirring constantly, until well incorporated. Add the hens and salt and mix well. Bring to a boil. Decrease the heat to medium and cook, covered, until the hens are tender and the sauce is thick and glazed, about 25 minutes. Transfer to a heated platter and serve immediately.

ROYAL CORNISH HEN BIRIYANI
with Raisins and Almonds

Shahi Biriyani

After Tandoori chicken, biriyani is the most popular preparation in Indian and Pakistani restaurants. Biriyani is best served immediately after cooking, while the mint and saffron perfumes are at their peak. For added richness, sprinkle 4 tablespoons heavy cream over the rice before covering and baking.

SERVES 8 TO 10

2 cups raw basmati rice

$^1/_2$ teaspoon saffron threads, lightly crushed

$^1/_4$ cup milk

1 tablespoon minced mint leaves

2 tablespoons melted *usli ghee* (page 185)

1 recipe Royal Braised Cornish Hens (page 110)

$^1/_4$ cup raisins, dark and/or light, for garnish

$^1/_4$ cup toasted pine nuts or almonds, for garnish

Silver leaf, for garnish (optional)

1. Wash the rice and soak in water to cover by an inch for at least 30 minutes or up to 2 hours. Combine the saffron and milk in another bowl and soak for 30 minutes.

2. Preheat the oven to 300° and place a rack in the middle position.

3. Bring 3 quarts of salted water to a boil in a deep pot. Drain the rice and add to the boiling water, stirring to prevent settling. Bring the water to a boil again and cook for exactly 4 minutes. Drain the rice well in a large sieve and transfer to a heated bowl. Add the saffron milk, mint, and *usli ghee* and mix lightly.

4. Spread half of the rice in a heavy ovenproof casserole. Distribute the hens on top and cover with the remaining rice. Cover the casserole tightly with aluminum foil and place the lid on top. Bake for 35 minutes, or until heated through. Carefully transfer the *biriyani* to a heated platter. Garnish with the raisins and nuts and decorate with the silver leaf. Serve immediately.

CORNISH HEN VINDALOO

Vindaloo

Vindaloo is a hot and spicy dish generally associated with Goa, the former Portuguese colony on India's western coast. Vindaloos come in a range of spiciness, from moderate to blisteringly hot—the secret to their deliciousness in the spicing. Sweet cinnamon, cloves, anise, and shallots not only round out the flavors, but temper the heat to a very pleasant spark. Vindaloo is traditionally served with plain rice, although a mild pilaf is also a nice accompaniment, as is some bread and a fruity yogurt salad.

SERVES 4

2 (1 $^1/_4$- to 1 $^3/_4$-pound) Cornish hens

3 tablespoons mustard oil (page 182) or vegetable oil

$^3/_4$ cup finely chopped shallots

1 tablespoon minced garlic

2 teaspoons ground red pepper

$^3/_4$ teaspoon ground cinnamon

$^1/_2$ teaspoon ground cloves

$^1/_4$ teaspoon ground anise

1 tablespoon tomato paste

1 tablespoon prepared mustard

1 teaspoon maple syrup

1 $^1/_2$ cups water

Coarse salt

1. Split the hens in half and remove the skin and all visible fat. Heat 1 tablespoon of the oil in a large heavy nonstick sauté pan over high heat. If you are using the mustard oil, let it smoke for a moment to rid it of its pungency. Decrease the heat, add the hens, and cook, turning, until they lose their pink color, about 5 minutes. Using a slotted spoon, remove them from the pan and transfer to a bowl.

2. Add the remaining 2 tablespoons oil to the pan. Add the shallots and garlic and cook, stirring occasionally, until the shallots are browned, about 10 minutes. Stir in the red pepper, cinnamon, cloves, and anise. Add the tomato paste, mustard, maple syrup, water, hens, and salt to taste. Bring to a boil.

3. Lower the heat and cook, covered, for 35 minutes, or until the hens are very tender. *(The vindaloo may be prepared ahead and refrigerated for up to 4 days or frozen. In fact, the flavors improve with standing. It is also easier to remove the excess fat, which congeals at the top, when the dish is cold.)*

4. Transfer the vindaloo to a warm dish and serve.

Variations

PORK VINDALOO

Use 4 pork chops (about 2 pounds), trimmed of excess fat, in place of the Cornish hens. Increase the cooking time to $1^1/_4$ hours.

BEEF OR LAMB VINDALOO

Use $1^1/_2$ pounds boneless lean beef or lamb, cut into $1^1/_2$-inch pieces, in place of the hens. Increase the cooking time to $1^3/_4$ hours.

VEGETABLE VINDALOO

Replace the hens with 6 cups mixed vegetables, such as cauliflower, carrots, green beans, green peas, turnips, eggplant, and/or potatoes, cut into 1 by 2-inch pieces.

ROAST DUCK
with Cinnamon-Plum Glaze

Battak Roosht

Gloriously glazed to a rich mahogany, this cinnamon-laced roast duck can form the centerpiece of the most Western of dinners. Traditionally the roast does not have a watercress garnish, but I like to use it to contrast the sweet flavor and add more complexity. It goes very well with Green Pea Pilaf (page 61) or Saffron Pilaf (page 64).

SERVES 4

1 (4- to 5-pound) duck, excess fat removed

Coarse salt and black pepper

2 tablespoons unsalted butter

1 cup (about 15) shallots, peeled

2 (3-inch) sticks cinnamon

4 large purple plums, sliced

$^1/_3$ cup damson plum jam

$^1/_4$ teaspoon ground cinnamon

$^1/_4$ teaspoon ground ginger

1 (6- to 7-ounce) bunch watercress, for garnish (optional)

1. Preheat the oven to 425°.

2. Rinse the duck and pat dry with paper towels. Rub salt and pepper all over the duck, inside and out.

3. Melt the butter in a large heavy nonstick sauté pan over medium-high heat. Add the shallots and the cinnamon sticks and fry, tossing frequently, until the shallots are lightly browned, about 10 minutes. Add the plums and cook, tossing, until coated with butter and heated through, about 1 minute. Spoon the cinnamon-plum-shallot mixture into the cavity of the duck. Sew or skewer closed.

4. Pour 1 cup water into a shallow roasting pan. Set the duck on its side on a rack in the pan. Roast for 45 minutes, turning every 15 minutes, first to the second side and then breast up.

5. Decrease the oven temperature to 350°. Combine the plum jam with the ground cinnamon and ginger. Brush the duck with some of the spiced jam. Continue to roast, turning occasionally and brushing with plum jam, until the duck is deep mahogany colored and tender, about 1 hour.

6. To serve, carve the duck into 4 portions and scoop out the stuffing. Spread the watercress on a serving platter. Arrange the duck in the center and surround with shallots, plum slices, and cinnamon sticks. Serve immediately.

MEAT

THE Moghuls are credited with introducing some of the greatest meat dishes of Indian cooking. Lamb Curry with Apricots, Lamb with Spinach, and Kid Braised in a Fragrant Cream Sauce are just few examples. The meat most frequently used in Indian cooking is lamb or goat meat. This is because the religious taboos of the Hindus prevent them from eating beef, and those of the Muslims prevent them from eating pork.

Except for Beef Frazer, which is made with leftover roast beef, dishes in this chapter can be prepared ahead and refrigerated. In fact, the flavor improves with standing. They can also be frozen. Defrost slowly in the refrigerator before reheating.

You can use any cut of meat as long as the skin and fat is trimmed away so that flavorings can penetrate into the meat. Although not traditional, pork and veal can be substituted in recipes calling for lamb or beef.

LAMB CURRY

Gosht Masala

The most popular of all curries, this one can be enjoyed with a simple bowl of rice or some bread. In place of lamb, you can substitute beef, veal, pork, or goat meat. Accompany with Green Pea Pilaf (page 61) or Flaky Parsley Pinwheel Bread (page 43) and Cool Cucumber and Yogurt Salad (page 154).

SERVES 4

1¹/₂ pounds boneless lean leg of lamb, cut into 1¹/₂-inch pieces

3 tablespoons vegetable oil

2 cups finely chopped onion

1 tablespoon grated fresh ginger

2 teaspoons minced garlic

2 teaspoons ground cumin

1 tablespoon ground coriander

¹/₂ teaspoon ground red pepper

1 tablespoon paprika

1 teaspoon turmeric

1 cup puréed tomato

Coarse salt

¹/₃ cup chopped cilantro leaves and tender stems

1. Heat a heavy nonstick saucepan over high heat. Add the lamb and 1 tablespoon of the oil. Sear the meat, turning and tossing, until nicely browned all over. Transfer the meat to a plate.

2. Add the remaining 2 tablespoons oil and the onion to the pan and cook, stirring often, until the onion is browned, about 15 minutes. Stir in the ginger, garlic, cumin, coriander, red pepper, paprika, and turmeric and cook for 3 minutes more. Add the tomato purée, lamb, salt to taste, and enough water to fully cover the meat, about 1¹/₂ cups. Bring to a boil. Decrease the heat and simmer, covered, for 1¹/₂ hours, or until the meat is cooked and very tender. Let the curry rest for at least 30 minutes and reheat it before serving. *(This dish may be made ahead and refrigerated for up to 3 days or frozen. In fact, the flavors improve with standing. If frozen, defrost and reheat slowly until piping hot.)*

3. Sprinkle with cilantro and serve.

Variations

LAMB CURRY WITH APRICOTS

Sauté 1 pound ripe apricots, peeled, pitted, and cut into thick wedges, in 1 tablespoon vegetable oil in a large sauté pan until streaked with brown and glazed, about 6 minutes. Arrange the apricots on top of the curry before serving.

LAMB CURRY WITH OKRA

Fry 4 ounces okra, stemmed and left whole, in 2 tablespoons oil in a large sauté pan until lightly browned and partially cooked, about 10 minutes. Add to the curry during the last 10 minutes of cooking.

LAMB CURRY WITH POTATOES

Add 4 to 6 scrubbed small waxy or new potatoes during the last 30 minutes of cooking.

LAMB CURRY WITH ZUCCHINI

Add 2 medium zucchini, diced into $1/2$ by 1-inch pieces, during the last 15 minutes of cooking.

LAMB
with Spinach

Saag Gosht

Spinach is eaten extensively in India; it is inexpensive and available year round. It is used to flavor breads and yogurt salads, to make dumplings and soup, or is stir-fried in a fragrant oil. In this dish, it is used to enhance the sauce. In place of spinach, you can substitute an equal quantity of another green, or a combination of other greens, such as mustard greens, Swiss chard, or beet tops. Accompany the curry with bread or rice.

SERVES 4

1 packed cup chopped cooked spinach, fresh or frozen

3 tablespoons vegetable oil

1/2 cup finely chopped onion

2 teaspoons *Garam Masala* (page 7) or ground cumin

1 to 2 teaspoons minced green chiles (optional)

1 recipe Lamb Curry (page 118)

1. Squeeze the spinach to remove excess moisture. Set aside.

2. Heat the oil in a large sauté pan. When the oil is hot, add the onion and cook until brown, about 8 minutes. Stir in the *Garam Masala* and chiles. Add the spinach and sauté for 3 minutes. *(The spinach mixture may be made ahead and refrigerated up to 2 days. Stir the spinach into the curry just before serving.)*

3. Add the seasoned spinach to the curry, stir well to mix, and serve.

CURRY
with Brussels Sprouts

Mutton Curry

This curry is an Anglo-Indian classic from the town of Ootacamund (affection-ately known as Ooty) in the Blue Mountain range of southern India. Brussels sprouts, introduced by the British in the nineteenth century, grow abundantly there. They are a pleasant addition to curry, giving it a very earthy wholesome taste. Mixed green salad and bread will complete the meal. For hot curry, add minced green chiles to taste with the cream.

SERVES 4

1 pound boneless lean lamb, cut into 1¹/₂-inch pieces

3 tablespoons all-purpose flour

¹/₄ cup vegetable oil

1 cup finely chopped shallots

2 tablespoons Curry Powder (page 6)

1 tablespoon prepared mustard

1 cup Chicken Stock (page 25)

Coarse salt

1 pound Brussels sprouts, trimmed

¹/₄ cup heavy cream

Black pepper

1. Dust the meat with flour. Heat 2 tablespoons of the oil in a large heavy nonstick sauté pan over high heat. Add the meat and sauté, turning, until browned on all sides, about 3 minutes. Transfer the meat to a plate.

2. Add the remaining 1 tablespoon oil to the pan along with the shallots and Curry Powder. Cook, stirring, until the spices give off an aroma. Return the meat to the pan. Add the mustard, stock, and salt to taste and bring to a boil. Decrease the heat and simmer, covered, stirring occasionally, for 1 hour. Fold in the brussels sprouts and continue to cook for 25 minutes more, or until they are tender but still firm. Stir in the cream.

3. Sprinkle with black pepper and serve.

SPICED GOAN ROAST PORK
with Jaggery Glaze

Lai Thao

When it comes to pork, no one in India loves it more or prepares better than the Goan Christians of Bombay. Here is a festive roast pork recipe that my second cousin, Sacho D'Souza, serves at Easter. Lemon Pilaf (page 58), Peach Chutney with Walnuts and Saffron (page 163), and Cauliflower with Nigella in Ginger Oil (page 135) would be perfect with this preparation.

SERVES 8

1 (3- to 3^1/2-pound) boneless pork loin roast, tied at 1-inch intervals

SPICE RUB

2 tablespoons minced garlic

1 tablespoon crushed or grated fresh ginger

2 teaspoons mustard seeds, crushed

2 teaspoons ground cinnamon

^{1}/2 teaspoon ground cloves

1 teaspoon turmeric

1^1/2 teaspoons cayenne pepper

^{1}/2 teaspoon black pepper

2 teaspoons coarse salt

2 tablespoons red wine vinegar

3 tablespoons clarified butter

^{1}/4 cup powdered jaggery or unsulfured molasses

^{3}/4 cup water

1 tablespoon cornstarch dissolved in 3 tablespoons red wine or water

1 teaspoon lemon juice

^{1}/4 cup dried red currants or raisins

1 tablespoon finely julienned fresh ginger

Coarse salt and black pepper

1. Place the pork in a shallow dish and prick all over with a fork. Combine all the ingredients for the spice rub mixture and spread evenly over the pork. Cover and marinate in the refrigerator for 2 hours. *(The pork may be refrigerated for up to 2 days but should be taken out at least 30 minutes before cooking, or additional time should be allowed during cooking.)*

2. Preheat the oven to 500° and place a rack in the middle position.

3. Place the pork, fat side up, on a rack set in a roasting pan. Roast, uncovered, for 15 minutes. Decrease the heat to 350°, baste the pork with the clarified butter, and continue to roast for 1 hour.

4. Sprinkle 3 tablespoons of the jaggery over the roast and continue cooking for 30 minutes longer, or until a meat thermometer inserted in the center registers 160°. The jaggery should have melted and formed a glaze. Remove the roast from the oven and let it rest for 15 minutes on a cutting board before slicing.

5. Place the roasting pan on the stovetop over medium heat and pour in the water. Scrape the bottom of the pan to loosen the drippings. Bring to a boil for 2 minutes, then stir in the cornstarch solution. Stir in the remaining 1 tablespoon jaggery and the lemon juice, currants, ginger, and salt and pepper to taste.

6. To serve, remove and discard the trussing strings, cut the meat into thin slices, and arrange on a heated serving platter. Spoon some of the gravy over the pork and serve the rest on the side.

Variations

SPICED GOAN ROAST CHICKEN

Substitute 2 small fryers, weighing about 2¹/₂ pounds each, in place of the pork. Remove the skin and cut the chicken into serving pieces. Decrease the cooking time at the 350° temperature to 35 minutes.

SPICED GOAN ROASTED VEGETABLES

Use 2 pounds potatoes, 1 pound eggplant, and 1 pound Brussels sprouts in place of the pork. Partially peel and cut the potatoes into 1¹/₂-inch pieces, the eggplant into 2-inch pieces, and trim the Brussels sprouts. Toss the vegetables in the spice rub and the butter. Spread the vegetables on a baking sheet and roast, decreasing the cooking time at the 350° temperature to 35 minutes.

KID BRAISED IN
a Fragrant Cream Sauce

Aab Gosht

This Moghul specialty from Pakistan is an elegant, rich dish generally reserved for company. Goat meat is first braised in an aromatic cream sauce, then dressed with garlic-herb butter. Veal or lamb may be substituted for the goat meat. This dish is best served with a fragrant pilaf such as Peach and Walnut Basmati Pilaf (page 59) or Saffron Pilaf (page 64).

SERVES 4 TO 6

1 cup light cream

1 cup chopped onion

3 tablespoons blanched almonds

1 teaspoon ground cardamom

$1/4$ teaspoon grated nutmeg

$1/4$ teaspoon ground cloves

$1/4$ teaspoon ground anise

$1^1/2$ pounds boneless goat meat or veal, cut into 1-inch pieces

Coarse salt

2 tablespoons *usli ghee* (page 185) or clarified butter

1 teaspoon minced garlic

$1/2$ teaspoon black pepper

2 tablespoons minced mint

2 tablespoons minced cilantro leaves and tender stems

$1/2$ cup heavy cream (optional)

1. Combine the light cream, onion, and almonds in the workbowl of an electric blender or food processor. Process until liquefied. Mix in the cardamom, nutmeg, cloves, and anise.

2. Combine the puréed mixture with the meat in a large, heavy nonstick saucepan, season with salt, and bring to a boil. Lower the heat and simmer, partially covered, for 1 hour, or until the meat is tender and the sauce is thick enough to coat the meat. Stir often to prevent sticking and burning.

3. Heat the *usli ghee* in a small frying pan over medium-high heat until hot. Add the garlic, black pepper, mint, and cilantro. As soon as the garlic releases aroma, remove the pan from heat. Immediately pour the herb mixture over the meat. Add the cream, mix well, and serve.

DRY-COOKED SPICY GROUND BEEF

Sookha Keema

Dry-cooked ground meat is one of the most basic Moghul preparations. It may be served as a main dish in its own right or be made more substantial by combining it with cooked vegetables such as potatoes, sweet potatoes, turnips, or plantain. It is the basis for the classic filling for the Moghul stuffed bread (page 45). For a quick sandwich, stuff pita pockets or taco shells with the beef, topping it with sliced tomatoes and lettuce. The following recipe, developed in my cooking school, is quick, easy, and light. It produces just as good results as one using the conventional method.

SERVES 4

1¹/₂ pounds lean ground sirloin or round

3 tablespoons vegetable oil

4 teaspoons ground coriander

2 teaspoons ground cumin

1 teaspoon turmeric

¹/₂ teaspoon ground red pepper

1¹/₂ cups finely chopped onion

2 tablespoons minced garlic

2 tablespoons grated or crushed fresh ginger

2 cups chopped tomatoes, fresh or canned

2 cups water

Coarse salt

1. Heat a heavy saucepan over medium-high heat. Add the beef and cook, stirring, until it is no longer pink and begins to brown. Transfer to a colander, drain, and return to the pan.

2. Add the oil, coriander, cumin, turmeric, red pepper, onion, garlic, and ginger. Cook, stirring, until the onion looks soft and glazed, about 10 minutes. Add the tomatoes, water, and salt to taste and bring to a boil. Decrease the heat and simmer, uncovered, until all the moisture evaporates, about 30 minutes. Check periodically and stir to prevent sticking and burning.

3. Serve immediately or set aside for other uses.

NOTE: For a smoother texture, transfer the cooked beef to a food processor and process briefly. Do not overprocess as it will turn into an unpleasant paste.

MOGHUL GROUND MEAT STEW

Keema

This spicy Indian stew is similar in appearance to the Mexican chili. It is a great party dish since it is easy to make in quantity and it keeps well at room temperature. The texture of Keema *can be lumpy and coarse. If you prefer it less rustic, use a potato masher to break up the lumps of ground beef when preparing the dry-cooked beef. The stew is generally accompanied with Indian Salsa (page 164) and Deep-Fried Puffy Bread (page 38) or Mint Rice (page 63).*

SERVES 4

1 recipe Dry-Cooked Spicy Ground Beef
   (page 125)

1 cup tomato purée

1. Prepare the beef through step 2 of the recipe. Stir in the tomato purée and as much water as needed to make a thick chili-like mixture.

2. Reheat and serve hot.

Variation

For a richer, creamy *keema,* use milk or heavy cream in place of the water.

GROUND MEAT
with Smoked Eggplant

Keema Baigan

For the purist, here is Keema *made the traditional way, in which the onions are browned before the meat and spices are added. For a special twist, I have added smoky roasted eggplant to the finished* Keema; *it lends flavor and body to the sauce. You can substitute lamb, goat meat, pork, or chicken for the beef. This* Keema *is also delicious made with venison, buffalo, or moose meat. Serve it with a simple bread like* chapati *(page 32) or with Mint Rice (page 63).*

SERVES 4

2 medium eggplants (about 1¹/₂ pounds)

1 tablespoon lemon juice

2 cups chopped onion

1 tablespoon chopped garlic

¹/₄ cup vegetable oil

1 pound lean ground sirloin or round

2 cups water

1 tablespoon *Garam Masala* (page 7)

Coarse salt

2 cups peeled and chopped tomatoes

2 teaspoons grated fresh ginger

¹/₄ cup chopped cilantro leaves and tender stems

1. Place the eggplant on a gas burner, at first stem side up then laying them on their sides, turning them every minute until they are fully charred and very soft, about 20 minutes. When cool enough to handle, carefully scrape the charred skin off. Rinse quickly under cold running water to wash away any clinging charred pieces, and drain. Coarsely chop the pulp and put in a bowl. Stir in the lemon juice and set aside. *(The eggplant may be made ahead and refrigerated for up to 2 days or frozen. Defrost before proceeding with step 3.)*

2. Put the onion, garlic, and oil in a large heavy saucepan. Cook over medium-high heat, stirring occasionally, until the onion is browned, about 15 minutes. Add the ground beef and continue to cook until it loses its pink color. Add the water and bring to a boil. Lower the heat and cook,

(continued)

covered, until the meat is tender and the sauce thickened, about 25 minutes. *(The meat may be refrigerated for up to 2 days or frozen. Defrost before proceeding with step 3.)*

3. Stir in the *Garam Masala*, salt to taste, tomatoes, ginger, cilantro, and eggplant. Heat thoroughly and serve.

NOTE: To roast eggplants in the oven, place them in a shallow baking dish and bake in a preheated 425° oven for 45 minutes, or until the eggplants are soft and limp and their skin entirely wrinkled.

BEEF FRAZER

Jhal frazi

Named after Colonel Frazer, an important figure of the British Raj, this dish is a sauté of leftover roast beef with vegetables. It makes a great buffet dish and is also good for lunch, accompanied by plain rice and a vegetable like Curried Eggplant with Chutney (page 136).

SERVES 2

3/4 pound leftover roast beef

1 teaspoon ground cumin

2 teaspoons Curry Powder (page 6)

4 tablespoons unsalted butter

4 scallions, trimmed and shredded, green and white parts

1 cup thin tomato wedges with skin

2 teaspoons prepared mustard

1/4 cup Chicken Stock (page 25) or water

Black pepper

2 tablespoons chopped cilantro leaves and tender stems

1. Cut the beef into 1-inch cubes. Sprinkle with the cumin and Curry Powder and rub in. Heat the butter in a large sauté pan over medium-high heat. When the butter melts, add the beef and scallions and sauté, turning, for 4 minutes, or until the beef is warmed through and begins to brown.

2. Increase the heat to high and add the tomatoes. Stir the mustard into the stock and pour over the beef. Cook until the tomatoes begin to soften, about 4 minutes.

3. Transfer to a platter, sprinkle with black pepper and cilantro, and serve.

VEGETABLES, LEGUMES, EGGS, AND CHEESE

WITH over 700 million practicing vegetarians in India, it should come as no surprise that India is the ruling champion when it comes to vegetable cooking. Fresh, seasonal vegetables are prepared in myriad ways with intricate spicing and seasonings. Often the vegetables are flavored with only one or two spices to lend just a teasing fragrance. The vegetables are cooked in hot, spice-infused oil. Each Indian kitchen has its own preferred flavors and techniques, but generally speaking, those in the north commonly use cumin; those in the east, mustard; those in the south, kari; and those in the west, ajowan. Just about any vegetable can be prepared the Indian way; the popular ones are cauliflower, eggplant, potato, squash, green beans, and greens. Legumes, eggs, and homemade cheese, popular ingredients of the Indian vegetarian diets, are enjoyed by all.

GREEN BEANS
in Fenugreek Oil

Sem Bhaji

These green beans are flavored in style of Assam, where vegetables are often cooked in oil flavored with fenugreek, garlic shoots, and chiles. My maternal grandparents, who settled in Burma near the Assam border, particularly liked this dish made with green beans or with spinach, the traditional choices. Wonderful with tandoori meats, the beans are also good served cold with drinks.

SERVES 4

1 pound green beans

1 small bunch garlic shoots, or
　　6 scallions

1 tablespoon vegetable oil

¹/₄ teaspoon fenugreek seeds

¹/₂ teaspoon turmeric

¹/₂ teaspoon finely chopped
　　green chiles

Coarse salt

¹/₃ cup water

1. Trim the green beans and rinse in cold water. Trim the garlic shoots and cut into 4-inch-long pieces, then quarter each lengthwise.

2. Heat the oil in a large heavy sauté pan over high heat. Add the fenugreek seeds and cook until they turn very dark brown, about 1 minute. Add the green beans, garlic shoots, turmeric, and chiles. Fry the vegetables, turning and tossing, until lightly browned, about 5 minutes. Sprinkle with salt to taste and the water.

3. Decrease the heat and cook, covered, until soft, about 10 minutes. If the vegetables look a little moist, uncover and boil rapidly until dried and glazed.

4. Serve hot, at room temperature, or chilled.

Variation

For a real treat, substitute ramps (spicy baby leeks) for the garlic shoots. Ramps can be purchased in specialty produce markets in the spring.

GREEN BEANS AND CARROTS
with Mustard Seeds

Kottaivaraika Porial

Indian cooks prepare porial *using different varieties of green beans, such as butter, yard, and cluster. The cooking technique and time are the same no matter what kind of bean you choose. For variety, substitute yellow turnip in place of the carrots.* Porial *is good served hot, at room temperature, or cold.*

SERVES 4

2 tablespoons vegetable oil

3/4 teaspoon black mustard seeds

2 dried red chiles

2 teaspoons white gram beans

24 kari leaves, fresh or dried

3/4 teaspoon turmeric

1/2 teaspoon ground red pepper

3/4 pound green beans, trimmed and cut into 1-inch pieces

1/2 pound carrots, peeled and cut into 1-inch matchsticks

1 teaspoon coarse salt

1 cup water

1/4 cup unsweetened grated coconut

1. Heat the oil in a large frying pan over medium-high heat. When the oil is hot, add the mustard seeds and chiles and cover the pan with the lid because the seeds will pop and spatter. When the sputtering subsides, uncover and add the white gram beans, kari leaves, turmeric, and red pepper. When the beans begin to color, add the green beans, carrots, salt, and water. Mix well and bring to a boil.

2. Decrease the heat and cook, covered, until the vegetables are tender, about 14 minutes. Uncover and continue cooking, turning and tossing, until the excess moisture evaporates. Check for salt and add more as needed. Add half of the coconut and stir-fry for 1 minute. Transfer to a heated platter and serve sprinkled with the remaining coconut.

BROCCOLI AND CARROTS
in Garlic-Turmeric Oil

Sabzi

This crisp sauté is great with fish, such as Steamed Fish in Herb Sauce (page 90). Since the dish may be served hot, cold, or at room temperature, it is perfect for a buffet or picnic. In India, vegetables cooked this way are usually served with flatbread to wrap around them.

SERVES 4

1 (1³/4-pound) bunch broccoli

2 medium carrots

3 tablespoons vegetable oil

10 large cloves garlic, peeled

¹/2 teaspoon turmeric

¹/2 teaspoon sugar

¹/2 lime

1. Cut the broccoli into spears, leaving long stems attached to the florets and peel the stems. Peel and slice the carrots lengthwise into ¹/4-inch-wide strips.

2. Bring a large pot of water to a boil and add the broccoli and carrots. Blanch for about 2 minutes, drain, rinse under cold running water, and drain again.

3. Heat the oil in a large sauté pan over medium-high heat. Add the garlic cloves and sauté over medium heat until golden, about 6 minutes. Add the broccoli, carrots, and turmeric and sauté, stirring frequently, until the vegetables soften, about 6 minutes. Sprinkle with sugar and continue to sauté until the vegetables are lightly browned, about 2 minutes more.

4. To serve, pick the broccoli and carrots up with tongs and arrange them in a bouquet on a serving platter. Scatter the leftover garlic from the pan on top and sprinkle with lime juice. Serve hot, at room temperature, or chilled.

CAULIFLOWER
with Nigella in Ginger Oil

Adrak Gobhi

Of all the vegetables, it seems Indians like cauliflower the most. In this prepara-tion, it is lightly spiced, then sautéed in a ginger-infused oil. This gives the dish an herbal fragrance without overpowering the delicate flavor of the cauliflower. It can be served with any spicy dish.

SERVES 4

1 (1¹/₂-pound) head cauliflower

2 tablespoons vegetable oil

2 tablespoons julienned fresh ginger

3/4 teaspoon nigella seeds or
    cumin seeds

¹/₂ teaspoon turmeric

¹/₂ cup water

Coarse salt

1. Separate the cauliflower into small florets, cutting them with a knife if necessary. Peel the cauliflower stem and slice it into ¹/₄-inch-thick rounds. Wash the cauliflower pieces in cold running water and drain.

2. Heat the oil in a large sauté pan over medium heat. When the oil is hot, add the ginger and let it sizzle in the oil for 1 minute. Add the nigella seeds, turmeric, and cauliflower. Sauté, turning and tossing, until evenly coated with the spices, about 3 minutes.

3. Stir in the water and salt to taste. Decrease the heat and cook, covered, until the cauliflower is fully cooked but still firm, about 10 minutes. Uncover, increase the heat, and stir-fry until any excess moisture has evaporated and the cauliflower looks glazed.

Variation

For a hotter dish, stir in 2 chopped green chiles and/or ¹/₄ teaspoon ground red pepper along with the nigella and turmeric.

CURRIED EGGPLANT
with Chutney

Bhona Baigan

An old Anglo-Indian favorite, this curry-flavored eggplant is sweet and savory at the same time, perfect with tandoori meats, simple grilled chicken, or sautéed fish. I also like to make a sandwich of it with lettuce and tomato for a satisfying vegetarian snack. The dish is good both hot and at room temperature.

SERVES 4

2 large eggplants (about 2 pounds)

1 medium onion, peeled and cut into ¼-inch slices

2 teaspoons Curry Powder (page 6)

¼ teaspoon ground ginger

3 tablespoons vegetable oil

2 teaspoons lemon juice

Coarse salt

2 tablespoons Sweet Mango Chutney (page 162) or storebought

1. Bring a large pot of water to a boil. Cut the eggplant into 1-inch cubes Add the eggplant cubes to the boiling water and blanch for 1 minute. Drain and put in a bowl. Add the onion, Curry Powder, and ginger. Toss to mix.

2. Heat the oil in a large sauté pan over high heat. Add the eggplant mixture and sauté, tossing frequently, for about 3 minutes. Decrease the heat and cook, uncovered, tossing, until the eggplant is tender, about 25 minutes. Turn off the heat and stir in the lemon juice, salt to taste, and chutney.

Variation

You can make this dish more substantial and elaborate by sautéing potatoes, zucchini, or summer squash along with the eggplant. Diced fresh tomatoes add another dimension of flavor, color, and texture if used as a garnish.

BENGALI-STYLE EGGPLANT
with *Panch Phoron* Spices

Began Sorshe

A popular eggplant preparation of the Bengalis, Began Sorshe *is made by cooking eggplant in a delightful mustard-infused sauce. Yogurt is folded in at the end to mellow the high notes of the spices. Accompany it with a rice dish.*

SERVES 4

2 medium eggplants (about 1¹/2 pounds)

2 teaspoons brown mustard seeds, ground into a powder

¹/2 teaspoon ground red pepper

12 kari leaves, thinly shredded (optional)

¹/4 cup water

¹/4 cup vegetable oil

1 tablespoon *Panch Phoron* (page 8)

4 whole cloves

4 whole cardamom pods

³/4 cup water

1 cup plain yogurt

Coarse salt and freshly ground black pepper

2 tablespoons chopped cilantro

2 green chiles, stemmed and sliced (optional)

1. Trim the eggplants and cut into 1¹/2-inch pieces. In a small bowl, stir together the mustard powder, red pepper, kari leaves, and water to form a paste.

2. In a large, heavy pan, heat the oil over medium-high heat. When the oil is hot, add the *Panch Phoron*, cloves, and cardamom. Cook, stirring, until the spices turn several shades darker, about 30 seconds. Add the mustard paste and stir for 1 minute. Fold in the eggplant. Pour the water over and cover the pan. Cook until the eggplant is tender, about 10 minutes. Uncover and continue cooking, stirring, until the excess moisture evaporates, about 5 minutes. Stir in the yogurt and salt and black pepper to taste. Cook only until the yogurt is heated through, about 1 minute. Transfer to a serving platter, sprinkle with cilantro and chiles, and serve hot or at room temperature.

HYDERABAD CHILES
Braised in Tamarind Sauce

Mirch ka Salan

This preparation is the specialty of Hyderabad, a city in the southern state of Andra Pradesh, known worldwide for its chiles. The dish's rich taste and visual appeal makes it ideal for banquet presentations. Serve hot with rice or bread.

SERVES 6

1¹/₂ pounds medium-hot chiles such as arbol, poblano, or Anaheim

¹/₄ cup vegetable oil

¹/₄ cup unsweetened coconut flakes

1 tablespoon sesame seeds

1 tablespoon chickpea flour

2 teaspoons white poppyseeds

1 to 3 teaspoons crushed red pepper flakes

1 teaspoon ground cumin

¹/₂ teaspoon turmeric

1 teaspoon mustard seeds

1 cup chopped onion

1 tablespoon grated fresh ginger

1 tablespoon chopped mint leaves

2 teaspoons minced garlic

Coarse salt

1 cup water

¹/₂ cup tamarind juice

1. Slit the peppers lengthwise. Heat 2 tablespoons of the oil in a frying pan over medium-high heat. Add the coconut, sesame seeds, chickpea flour, and poppyseeds. Fry until light caramel brown, about 7 minutes. Turn off the heat and stir in the red pepper, cumin, and turmeric. Transfer to a blender and, using a little water, grind to a paste.

2. Heat the remaining 2 tablespoons oil in the pan over medium-high heat. Add the mustard seeds and cover with the lid because the seeds will pop and spatter. When the sputtering subsides, add the chiles and stir-fry for 5 minutes. Add the onion, ginger, mint, and garlic. Cook, stirring, for 5 minutes, or until caramelized. Add the spice paste, salt to taste, and water. Lower the heat and cook, partially covered, until the chiles are soft and the sauce is thick, about 8 minutes. Add the tamarind juice and cook for 1 minute before serving.

INDIAN WILTED SPINACH

Masial

A specialty of the central province of Bhopal, this wilted greens preparation is truly poor man's food. Freshly picked greens from the backyard are sautéed with chile and garlic. What gives the dish an added dimension of flavor is the mustard oil, a common cooking medium in the region. The dish, however, is delicious even without it. You can make this dish with other greens, such as chard, escarole, kale, and so forth. You should blanch these heartier greens before adding them to the hot oil, and increase the cooking time to 6 minutes.

SERVES 4

3 tablespoons mustard oil (page 182) or vegetable oil, or a combination

2 teaspoons finely chopped garlic

$^1/_2$ teaspoon crushed red pepper flakes

2 pounds fresh spinach, stemmed and carefully washed

Coarse salt and black pepper

1. If using mustard oil, heat it in a skillet over high heat. Let the oil smoke for a moment to rid it of its pungency. Add the garlic and red pepper and immediately top them with the spinach. Stir quickly and constantly until the spinach is wilted, about 3 minutes. Season with salt and pepper just as the spinach begins to wilt. Cook, stirring, until the spinach is tender, about 2 minutes more.

2. Transfer to a small dish and serve immediately.

CURRY-SCENTED MUSHROOMS

Khombi Bhaji

These garlicky, slightly spicy mushrooms are good as a nibble with drinks, as a sit-down first course, or even at breakfast with sausage and eggs. I particularly like them with a sautéed or fried dish like Parsi Breaded Shrimp in Green Paste (page 99) or Chicken Ginger Kebabs (page 72) and rice.

SERVES 4

2 tablespoons vegetable oil

1¹/₂ pounds white button mushrooms, halved or quartered if large

1 tablespoon Curry Powder (page 6)

1 tablespoon chopped garlic

¹/₄ teaspoon crushed red pepper flakes

¹/₄ teaspoon sugar

2 teaspoons lemon juice

2 tablespoons chopped cilantro leaves and tender stems

1. Heat the oil in a large heavy sauté pan over high heat. When the oil is hot, add the mushrooms and cook, turning and tossing, until lightly browned. Add the Curry Powder, garlic, red pepper, and sugar. Lower the heat and sauté, stirring, until the mushrooms are soft and glazed.

2. Sprinkle with lemon juice and cilantro and serve.

NOTE: Westerners do not usually associate mushrooms with Indian cooking. However, India does cultivate some of the finest morels available. For a more woodsy flavor, substitute fresh morels for the button mushrooms.

CUMIN POTATOES

Jeera Aloo

This is one the most popular everyday techniques for cooking vegetables in North India. It's so simple: cooked vegetables are pan-seared in a spice-infused oil. Any seasonal vegetable will work, although starchy vegetables like potatoes, sweet potatoes, taro root, and plantains are preferred. The potatoes are great at breakfast or with grilled meats. For a vegetarian meal, roll them in a flatbread or stuff them in pita pockets with lettuce and tomato slices.

SERVES 4

1¹/₂ pounds small waxy or new potatoes, unpeeled

1 tablespoon vegetable oil

1 teaspoon cumin seeds

¹/₂ teaspoon turmeric

Coarse salt

2 tablespoons minced cilantro leaves and tender stems

1. Boil the potatoes until tender but not cracked open. Drain. When cool enough to handle, quarter the potatoes, leaving the skin on.

2. Heat the oil in a large heavy nonstick sauté pan over medium-high heat. Add the cumin seeds and sauté until they turn several shades darker, about 1 minute. Add the turmeric, salt to taste, and potatoes and sauté, tossing frequently, until the potatoes are nicely browned, about 10 minutes.

3. Sprinkle with cilantro and serve hot, at room temperature, or cold.

Variation

Potatoes are a great foil for all kinds of variations on a theme. Experiment with different spices by substituting the cumin seed with mustard seed, nigella, ajowan, or fennel. The variations will all be delicious.

PAN-ROASTED POTATOES
with Five Spices

Aloo Bhona

This is one of the basic ways of cooking vegetables in eastern India. The vegetables are first cooked in a broth scented with Panch Phoron, *a blend of five spices, and then pan-roasted. Starchy vegetables, such as potatoes, are particularly well suited to this technique but you can use any seasonal vegetable, remembering to adjust the cooking time. For great flavor and color, use purple or Yukon Gold potatoes. For a hotter dish, stir in 1 teaspoon chopped chiles or $^1/_2$ teaspoon ground red pepper with the* Panch Phoron.

SERVES 4

2 tablespoons vegetable oil

$1^1/_2$ teaspoons *Panch Phoron* (page 8)

$1^1/_2$ pounds small waxy or new potatoes, left whole or halved

$^1/_4$ teaspoon powdered asafetida or minced garlic

1 cup water

Coarse salt and black pepper

Juice of $^1/_2$ lemon

1. Heat the oil in a large heavy nonstick pan over medium-high heat. Add the *Panch Phoron* and sauté until the spices turn several shades darker. Add the potatoes and sprinkle with asafetida.

2. Fry the potatoes, turning and tossing, until evenly coated with spices and lightly browned, about 5 minutes. Stir in the water and bring to a boil. Decrease the heat and cook, covered, until the potatoes are tender, about 20 minutes. Uncover and pan-roast until the excess moisture has evaporated and the potatoes look browned.

3. Season with salt and pepper to taste, sprinkle with lemon juice, and serve warm, at room temperature, or cold.

Variations ───────────────────────────────────

PAN-ROASTED BABY EGGPLANT WITH FIVE SPICES

Use 1^1/$_2$ pounds small Italian eggplant, halved or quartered with the stem, in place of the potatoes. Decrease the cooking time to 15 minutes.

PAN-ROASTED GREEN BEANS WITH FIVE SPICES

Use 1 pound fresh green butter beans, or asparagus, trimmed, in place of the potatoes. Decrease the cooking time to 15 minutes.

CHETTINAD LIMA BEANS

Kurma

The Chettiyars of Madurai cook this lovely rich-tasting stew of lima beans. Chickpeas, kidney beans, and black-eyed peas all work well in this recipe.

SERVES 6

1 cup whole raw cashew nuts

$1/2$ cup unsweetened coconut flakes

4 green chiles, stemmed

1 (1-inch) piece fresh ginger

1 teaspoon aniseed

1 teaspoon ground cumin

2 (10-ounce) packets frozen baby lima beans

$1/2$ teaspoon turmeric

1 teaspoon coarse salt

2 cups water

$1/4$ cup canola or vegetable oil

1 teaspoon brown mustard seeds

$1/2$ cup finely chopped onion

1 cinnamon stick

6 whole cloves

2 ripe tomatoes, peeled and chopped

4 tablespoons chopped cilantro

1. Combine $1/4$ cup of the cashews with the coconut, chiles, ginger, aniseed, and cumin in a blender. Grind, adding enough water to create a paste.

2. In a saucepan, boil the lima beans, turmeric, salt, and water over medium-high heat. Cook until soft, 5 minutes. Drain; reserve the water.

3. In a large, heavy nonstick pan, heat the oil over high heat. When the oil is very hot, add the mustard seeds and cover the pan with the lid because the seeds will pop and spatter. When the sputtering subsides, add the onion, cinnamon, cloves, and the remaining 3/4 cup cashew nuts. Cook, stirring, for 6 minutes, or until the onion is golden brown.

4. Add the tomatoes and cook until lightly fried, about 3 minutes. Add the coconut-spice paste and cook, stirring, until the oil begins to separate, about 2 minutes. Add the beans and reserved water and cook until the sauce is thick and glazed, about 10 minutes. Check for salt and add more as needed. Transfer to a heated platter and serve sprinkled with cilantro.

BRAISED CHICKPEAS
with Spicy Sauce

Chana Masala

Chickpeas in a spicy ginger-tomato sauce can be served at brunch or lunch accompanied by Deep-Fried Puffy Bread (page 38) and a sweet fruity chutney like the Peach Chutney with Walnuts and Saffron (page 163). Ajowan, a thyme-flavored spice, is usually added to chickpea preparations to help make them more digestible.

SERVES 4

3 tablespoons vegetable oil

2 teaspoons cumin seeds

$1/4$ teaspoon ajowan seeds or dried thyme

1 cup finely chopped onion

2 tablespoons grated fresh ginger

1 cup chopped tomato

2 tablespoons tomato paste

2 cups cooked or canned chickpeas, drained

Coarse salt and black pepper

GARNISH

$1/4$ cup finely chopped cilantro leaves and tender stems

$1/4$ cup finely chopped onion

1 tablespoon chopped green chiles

1. Heat the oil in a large pan over medium-high heat. Add the cumin, ajowan, onion, and ginger. Cook, stirring often, until the onion turns light brown, about 8 minutes. Add the tomato, tomato paste, and chickpeas.

2. Lower the heat and simmer, covered, for 15 minutes, or until the flavors have blended and the sauce is very thick. Season with salt and sprinkle generously with black pepper. *(This dish may be made ahead and refrigerated for up to 4 days or frozen. Defrost thoroughly before reheating. Check the seasonings, and if necessary, add up to 2 teaspoons Garam Masala (page 7) to perk up the flavors.)*

3. Transfer to a warm dish and top with chopped cilantro and onions. Pass the chiles on the side.

FENNEL, TOMATO, AND WHITE BEAN STEW
with Lucknow Fennel Seeds

Koyambo

Here is lovely stew of spring fennel bulbs scented with delicate, sweet Lucknow fennel seeds. Inspired by my grandmother's Blue Mountain Stew recipe, this dish was developed by my assistant Micki Trager, a talented, creative cook. The stew is lovely accompanied by some bread or plain cooked rice.

SERVES 4 TO 6

1 cup white gram beans

4 cups water

$^1/_2$ teaspoon turmeric

4 medium ripe tomatoes, cored, seeded, and cut into eighths

15 kari leaves

3 tablespoons vegetable oil

$^1/_2$ teaspoon brown mustard seeds

$1^1/_2$ teaspoons Lucknow fennel seeds

1 tablespoon Curry Powder (page 6)

1 large fennel bulb, cut in half through the root end and sliced into $^1/_4$- to $^1/_2$-inch slices

1 large onion, cut in half and sliced into $^1/_4$-inch slices

2 to 3 hot green chiles, stemmed, seeded, and finely chopped

Coarse salt

1 to 2 tablespoons *usli ghee* (page 185), for garnish

$^1/_4$ cup chopped cilantro, for garnish

1. Rinse the beans and place in a large saucepan along with the water and turmeric. Bring to a boil over medium-high heat. Decrease the heat and simmer, partially covered, for 30 to 40 minutes. Stir occasionally so the beans do not stick to the bottom of the pan. When the beans are soft and tender, add the tomatoes and the kari leaves. Mix well. Remove about half the mixture and purée in a blender or food processor, then return to the pot.

2. In a large, heavy nonstick pan, heat the oil over high heat. When the oil is very hot, add the mustard seeds, lower the heat to medium, and cover the pan with the lid because the seeds will pop and spatter. When the sputtering subsides, add the fennel seeds and cook until they are a few shades darker, about 30 seconds. Add the Curry Powder and stir for a

few seconds. Add the fennel and onion and stir to coat thoroughly with the spices. Cook until the vegetables just begin to color, about 5 minutes.

3. Add the bean mixture to the vegetables and bring to a gentle boil over medium heat. Decrease the heat to low and cook, covered, until the fennel and onions are tender but not limp, about 10 minutes. Turn off the heat and add the green chiles and salt to taste. Mix well and serve topped with a drizzle of *usli ghee* and chopped cilantro.

NOTE: Fresh fennel is a remarkably versatile vegetable. It has the flavor and aroma of licorice, which becomes subtler and milder when cooked. Used raw, fennel's fresh, clean taste and crispness make it a perfect addition to salads. It also lends itself easily and very successfully to baking, grilling, and stewing. In this recipe, the fresh fennel perfumes the stew with its mild anise aroma while maintaining a firm yet tender texture. A perfect foil to the soothing, spiced *dal* mixture.

Variations

FENNEL, TOMATO, AND WHITE BEAN SOUP

Processed in a blender to a smooth purée and thinned with 1 cup chicken stock, coconut milk, or buttermilk, this recipe will make a refreshing soup, served either chilled or hot. A little garnish of toasted almonds adds a festive touch.

MOREL STEW

To create a very appealing woodsy stew, substitute 1/2 to 3/4 pound mushrooms for the fresh fennel. Fresh morels are a good choice since they are indigenous to India and their earthy flavor complements the turmeric-laced *dal*. If morels are not in season, you can use any variety of fresh, preferably wild, mushrooms. If you are using mushrooms, omit the Lucknow fennel seeds and increase the amount of brown mustard seeds to 1 teaspoon.

NEW DELHI SPICED LENTILS

Dal

Dal, a purée of lentils flavored with spices and herbs, is served with all traditional Indian meals. Typically used as a sauce, dal is spooned over rice or grilled meat to add moisture to the meal. Thinned with low-fat milk, buttermilk, or tomato juice, dal makes a refreshing soup. You can use yellow lentils, yellow split peas, or yellow mung beans in place of red lentils. Yellow mung beans will take about the same time to cook, yellow lentils and split peas twice as long.

SERVES 4

1¹/₄ cups red lentils

¹/₂ teaspoon turmeric

Coarse salt

SPICE BUTTER

3 tablespoons *usli ghee* (page 185) or vegetable oil

1 teaspoon cumin seeds

4 large cloves garlic, peeled and thickly sliced

¹/₄ teaspoon ground red pepper

¹/₄ cup finely chopped cilantro leaves and tender stems

1. Put the lentils and turmeric in a saucepan. Add 3 cups water and bring to a boil. Decrease the heat and simmer, partially covered, until tender, about 20 minutes. Stir a few times during cooking to keep the lentils from sticking to the pan and burning. Add more water if necessary. Turn off the heat. The consistency should be like pea soup; if not, add more water. Add salt to taste, cover, and set aside.

2. Heat the *usli ghee* in a small frying pan over medium-high heat. Add the cumin seeds and sauté until they turn several shades darker. Add the garlic and red pepper. Sauté until the garlic turn golden, about 1 minute.

3. Transfer the lentils to a warm dish. Pour the spice-infused butter over the lentils. Sprinkle with cilantro and serve.

CURRIED LENTILS
with Tomatoes and Zucchini

Sambaar Dal

Packed with vegetables, this dal *is like a hearty stew or ragout, a one-dish meal. Flavorings in this* dal *are kept to a minimum so that the natural flavors of the lentils and basmati rice with which it is generally served are not masked. You could also serve it with Semolina Pilaf (page 65).*

SERVES 4

1 cup yellow lentils or yellow split peas

$1/2$ teaspoon turmeric

Coarse salt

1 cup chopped tomatoes

SPICED VEGETABLES

2 tablespoons vegetable oil

2 teaspoons Curry Powder (page 6)

2 teaspoons ground coriander

1 cup chopped shallots

1 cup chopped zucchini

$1/4$ cup chopped cilantro leaves and tender stems

1. Put the lentils and turmeric in a large saucepan. Add 3 cups water and bring to a boil. Decrease the heat and simmer, partially covered, until tender, about 35 minutes. Stir a few times during cooking to keep the lentils from sticking to the pan and burning. Add more water if necessary. Turn off the heat. Stir in the salt and tomatoes, cover, and set aside.

2. Heat the oil in a large skillet over medium heat. Add the Curry Powder, coriander, shallots, and zucchini. Sauté until the vegetables begin to brown, about 6 minutes. Decrease the heat and cook, covered, until the vegetables are tender, about 6 minutes. Add the vegetable mixture to the lentils and mix lightly. Check the seasonings and add salt if necessary. Heat through.

3. Sprinkle with cilantro and serve.

INDIAN-STYLE OMELET

Aamlait

Indians like everything spiced up. Not necessarily heavily, but a spice or two must be added to a dish for it be considered properly prepared. An omelet is no exception. Enriched with onion, tomato, chiles, and cilantro, this omelet is spicy and delicious. Choose the chiles, mild to hot, according to your taste.

SERVES 1

2 large eggs

2 tablespoons finely chopped red onion

2 tablespoons finely chopped tomato

1 to 2 teaspoons chopped green chiles

2 tablespoons chopped cilantro leaves and tender stems

Coarse salt

1 tablespoon *usli ghee* (page 185) or unsalted butter

1. Combine the eggs, onion, tomato, chiles, cilantro, and salt to taste in a bowl and beat until lightly frothy.

2. Heat the *usli ghee* in a large nonstick frying pan over medium-high heat. Add the egg mixture and spread, tilting and swirling, until it covers the entire bottom of the pan. Cook until the egg is set and the underside is lightly browned, about 1 1/2 minutes. Turn the omelet with a wide spatula and cook for 30 seconds, or until the second side is browned.

3. Transfer to a dinner plate and serve.

MASALA CHEESE SCRAMBLE

Paneer Bhorji

This is an Indian alternative to scrambled eggs, made with the Indian cheese paneer. *Filled with cilantro, chiles, and tomatoes,* bhorji *is light and refreshing. Accompany it with any Indian bread.*

SERVES 2

1 cup *paneer* (page 183), or 8 ounces farmer cheese or tofu

$^1/_8$ teaspoon turmeric mixed with 2 teaspoons water

Coarse salt

2 tablespoons *usli ghee* (page 185) or unsalted butter

$^1/_2$ teaspoon cumin seeds

$^1/_4$ cup finely chopped red onion

1 teaspoon grated or crushed ginger

1 to 2 teaspoons chopped green chiles

$^1/_2$ cup finely chopped tomatoes, drained

$^1/_4$ cup chopped cilantro leaves and tender stems or 12 kari leaves, chopped

1. Place the *paneer* in a bowl. Sprinkle with turmeric and salt to taste and set aside.

2. Heat the *usli ghee* in a large nonstick frying pan over medium-high heat. Add the cumin seeds and cook until the spice turns several shades darker. Add the onion, ginger, and chiles and cook until the onions are soft, about 3 minutes. Add the tomato and cheese and cook, stirring, until the seasonings are evenly distributed in the cheese, about 5 minutes.

3. Fold in the cilantro and serve.

YOGURT SALADS, CHUTNEYS, AND CONDIMENTS

Yogurt salads, combinations of yogurt, vegetables, fruits, and nuts, provide the moisture that may be lacking in such foods as grilled kebabs, roasts, and Tandoori Chicken. Raitas, as these yogurt salads are called, are mellow and cooling, hence an important adjunct to spicy Indian food. Raitas can also be puréed and served as a dip, such as Roasted Pepper Dip, or combined with cooked seafood or chicken in a salad like the Chicken and Roasted Pepper Chat.

Chutney, from the word *chatni*, which means licking good in Sanskrit, is a spicy condiment that appears at most India meals. It is a unique Indian combination of fruits, seasonings, vinegar, and sugar with nearly unlimited variations of ingredients and texture.

COOL CUCUMBER AND YOGURT SALAD

Kheera Raita

Flavored in the classic New Delhi style with roasted cumin and mint leaves, this subtle raita is an ideal accompaniment to all Moghul dishes, northern curries, and tandoori dishes.

SERVES 4

1 cup yogurt

1 teaspoon minced mint

Coarse salt and freshly ground black
   pepper

1 teaspoon sugar (optional)

2 medium cucumbers, peeled, seeded,
   and grated

1/4 teaspoon toasted cumin seeds

Whip the yogurt, mint, salt and pepper to taste, and sugar in a bowl until thoroughly blended. Stir in the cucumber and cumin seeds. Serve immediately or refrigerate.

BANANA-COCONUT YOGURT SALAD

Kela Raita

This cool banana raita is an all-time favorite at wedding receptions and banquets. Indian cooks would use the small finger bananas or red bananas, which are sweeter and firmer than regular bananas and hold their shape better in a sauce. For best result, use firm, just ripe bananas with no spots.

SERVES 4

2 cups yogurt

2 tablespoons sweetened grated
  coconut

$^1/_2$ teaspoon grated fresh ginger

$^1/_4$ teaspoon ground cardamom

1 teaspoon dried green peppercorns, or
  $^1/_4$ teaspoon ground white pepper

Coarse salt

2 bananas, thinly sliced

Whip the yogurt, coconut, ginger, cardamom, green peppercorns, and salt to taste in a bowl until thoroughly blended. Fold in the bananas. Refrigerate for at least 2 hours. Serve chilled.

ROASTED PEPPER
and Mint Yogurt Salad

Mirch Raita

This smoky raita can be served with any main dish or by itself accompanied by a stuffed Indian bread. It can be transformed into a very refreshing dip for fried food or into a chat, a hearty salad (see variations at the end of the recipe).

You may roast the peppers any way you like—on the grill, on a stovetop grill, over a gas flame, on a rack set on an electric burner, or under the broiler, as in step 2. You can do this ahead of time. In fact, you can prepare all the vegetables and refrigerate them, separately, for up to 1 day, then combine them with the yogurt, mint, and salt just before serving.

SERVES 4

2 medium green bell peppers

2 medium red bell peppers

2 small cucumbers, peeled, seeded, and thinly sliced

2 cups yogurt

2 tablespoons minced mint

2 tablespoons minced red onion

Coarse salt

1. Preheat the broiler.

2. Cut the peppers in half and place them, skin side up, under the broiler until charred. Transfer to a paper bag and fold it shut to let the peppers sweat, thus loosening the skin. When the peppers are cool enough to handle, rub the skin off with your fingers. Remove the core and seeds and discard.

3. Cut the peppers into $1/2$-inch pieces and put them in a bowl. Add all the other ingredients, including salt to taste, and mix until blended. Serve immediately or refrigerate.

Variations

SPICY ROASTED PEPPER SALAD

Substitute fresh ancho or poblano chiles for the green bell peppers.

ROASTED PEPPER DIP

Working in batches, purée the salad in a food processor or electric blender. Dilute with 1 cup of buttermilk.

CHICKEN AND ROASTED PEPPER CHAT

Fold 3/4 pound sliced cooked chicken, 1/2 cup chopped toasted pecans, 2 teaspoons prepared mustard, and 1 tablespoon mango chutney into the salad.

CARROT AND BLACKBERRY YOGURT SALAD
with Walnuts

Gajjar Raita

In the valley of Kashmir, this wonderful nutmeg-scented salad is made with freshly picked green walnuts that taste like truffle-scented chestnuts. If you are lucky enough to find them, use them instead of toasted walnuts. You can use toasted pecans, hazelnuts, and macadamia nuts in place of walnuts.

SERVES 4

1 cup plain yogurt

2 tablespoons maple syrup or honey

$1/4$ teaspoon grated nutmeg

$1/8$ teaspoon aniseed, crushed

$1/8$ teaspoon white pepper

$1/2$ pound carrots, peeled and finely diced

2 cups blackberries

1 cup chopped green or toasted walnuts

Whip the yogurt, maple syrup, nutmeg, aniseed, and white pepper in a bowl until thoroughly blended. Top with the carrots, blackberries, and walnuts. Fold the salad gently and serve.

Variation ——————————————————————————

Blanch the carrots in salted water, then cool completely before using.

MINT CHUTNEY

Podina Chatni

This fresh chutney, very fragrant and only slightly hot, is popular in Indian restaurants. It is perfect with fried food, roasted and grilled meats, and tandoori meats.

MAKES 1 CUP

²/₃ cup white wine vinegar

2 tablespoons maple syrup or sugar

4 green chiles, stemmed

1 (1-inch) cube fresh ginger, peeled

1 small green bell pepper, cored and chopped

1 lightly packed cup mint leaves

1 lightly packed cup cilantro leaves and tender stems

Put all the ingredients into the workbowl of an electric blender or food processor. Process, turning off and on and pushing the herbs down with a rubber spatula, until reduced to a sauce. Transfer to a small bowl and serve immediately or refrigerate.

COCONUT CHUTNEY

Narial Chatni

Imbued with the delicate sweetness of coconut and spices, this uncooked chutney goes well with all fish, seafood, and poultry dishes. What makes this recipe special is that you can use commercially available sweetened coconut flakes. As a result, you can put together the chutney in a matter of seconds. It is fine to purée cilantro stems, but not mint, as its stems tend to be fibrous.

SERVES 4

1 cup yogurt

1 packed cup sweetened coconut flakes

1 to 2 jalapeños, stemmed and sliced, with seeds

1 large clove garlic, peeled

1 ($\frac{1}{2}$-inch) piece fresh ginger, peeled

$\frac{1}{4}$ lightly packed cup cilantro leaves and tender stems

4 mint leaves

Coarse salt

1 teaspoon roasted cumin seeds

Combine the yogurt, coconut, jalapeños, garlic, ginger, coriander, mint, and salt to taste in an electric blender or a food processor and process until finely puréed. Transfer to a bowl. Check the seasoning and add more salt if necessary. Stir in the cumin seeds and serve immediately or refrigerate.

GARLIC-TOMATO CHUTNEY

Lassan Chatni

Try this hot garlic chutney with roasted or grilled meat or for a change of pace, spoon it over a pilaf or spread it on an Indian bread. The dried chiles are left in the chutney, but take care—they are too hot to eat.

MAKES 2 CUPS

1¹/₂ pounds tomatoes, peeled, seeded, and sliced

2 jalapeños, stemmed and minced, with seeds

1 tablespoon grated fresh ginger

¹/₄ cup vegetable oil

6 dried red chiles

1¹/₂ teaspoons *Panch Phoron* (page 8)

8 large garlic cloves, peeled and thickly sliced

Coarse salt

1. Combine the tomatoes, jalapeños, and ginger in a bowl.

2. Heat the oil in a heavy pan over medium-high heat. Add the dried chiles and fry until almost black, about 2 minutes. Reduce the heat to medium-low and add the *Panch Phoron* and garlic. Fry until the spices turn several shades darker and the garlic turns light brown, about 2 minutes. Add the tomato mixture and cook, uncovered, stirring occasionally, over low heat for 35 minutes, or until the chutney is thick and pulpy and the oil separates. Turn off the heat and stir in the salt to taste. Cool completely before using.

SWEET MANGO CHUTNEY

Aam Chatni

Make this classic mango chutney in early spring when unripe green mangoes appear at vegetable markets. It is astonishingly easy to prepare—all you do is combine all the ingredients and cook down the sauce to the consistency of jam. Mango chutney is sweetish hot and goes with any number of dishes. I particularly like it with lamb and chicken preparations.

MAKES 2 CUPS

SYRUP

1¹/₂ cups sugar

¹/₂ cup wine vinegar

1 teaspoon minced garlic

1 tablespoon ground ginger

3 tablespoons dry mustard

¹/₄ teaspoon ground cloves

¹/₄ teaspoon ground cinnamon

¹/₂ teaspoon ground red pepper

3 small firm, unripe mangoes
(1 pound), peeled and cut into
1-inch pieces

¹/₄ cup dark raisins

¹/₄ cup slivered almonds

1. Combine all the ingredients for the syrup in a stainless steel or enameled pan and bring to a boil over low heat, stirring often. Simmer until thick and syrupy, about 15 minutes.

2. Add the mango pieces and continue to cook for 10 minutes, or until the mango looks translucent. Turn off the heat. Add the raisins and almonds and serve warm or spoon into sterilized jars. When completely cool, cover and store. *(The chutney keeps well, for up to 3 weeks in the refrigerator.)*

PEACH CHUTNEY
with Walnuts and Saffron

Adoo Chatni

This peach chutney is a far cry from commercially prepared products. It is a delicious and irresistible example of the play of spices and flavor for which Indian cooking is justifiably famous. Seasoned with ginger, mustard, fennel, pepper, and saffron, it adds power and pizzazz to roasts and grills. Fresh nectarines and pineapple are both fine substitutes for the peaches. This chutney beautifully complements the Parsi Breaded Shrimp in Green Paste (page 99) as well as Tandoori Chicken (page 70).

MAKES 4 CUPS

2 pounds peaches, peeled, pitted, and
    sliced (4 cups)

1 cup white wine vinegar

1¹/₂ packed cups light brown sugar

2 tablespoons julienned fresh ginger

¹/₂ teaspoon saffron threads

1 teaspoon yellow mustard seeds

1 teaspoon fennel seeds

¹/₂ teaspoon crushed red pepper
    flakes

1 cup dark raisins

1 cup walnuts

1. Put the peaches in a large stainless steel or enameled pan. Add the vinegar and bring to a boil over medium-high heat. Cook the peaches until barely tender but not cooked through, about 7 minutes. Turn off the heat and let the peaches sit in the liquid for 5 minutes. Using a slotted spoon, transfer the fruit to a bowl, leaving the liquid in the pan.

2. Add the brown sugar, ginger, saffron, mustard, fennel, and red pepper to the liquid in the pan and bring back to a boil over high heat. Boil until the syrup turns sticky, about 12 minutes. Add the reserved peaches and continue to cook until the chutney looks thick and glazed like a jam, about 8 minutes. Turn off the heat and fold in the raisins and walnuts. Spoon the chutney into sterilized jars. Seal or cover and refrigerate. Let the chutney ripen for 1 day before serving.

INDIAN SALSA

Kachoomar

The relish kachoomar *is used primarily to add moisture to a meal. Not surprisingly, it goes well with stuffed breads, tandoori meats, roasts, and grilled chicken, lamb, and beef. Unlike Mexican salsa, which can range in heat from mild to dynamite-hot, Indian salsa is mild and fragrant. Particularly nice additions to the basic mix of tomatoes, chiles, cucumbers, and onions are daikon radish and Kirby cucumbers.*

SERVES 4

1 cup finely diced tomato, drained

1 tablespoon chopped green chiles

1 cup finely diced cucumber, preferably Kirby

1 cup finely diced red onion

1 cup finely diced radish, preferably daikon

1/2 cup chopped cilantro leaves and tender stems

1 tablespoon lemon juice

Put all the ingredients in a bowl, toss well to mix, and serve. *(The salsa can be prepared ahead and refrigerated for up to 1 day. Bring to room temperature before serving.)*

CUMIN-ONION BUTTER

Masala Ghee

Sometimes called baghar, *this very fragrant spice butter is used as a finishing flavor over lentil purées, soups, and Indian breads. It can also be served as a garnishing butter with pilafs and biriyani.*

MAKES ⅔ CUP

6 tablespoons *usli ghee* (page 185) or
    vegetable oil

2 teaspoons cumin seeds
2 cups chopped onion

1. Heat the *usli ghee* in a large frying pan over medium-high heat. Add the cumin seeds. When they turn several shades darker, add the onion and cook, stirring, until golden brown, about 15 minutes.

2. Transfer to a bowl and serve immediately. Or pour into a jar, let cool, cover, and refrigerate. *(The butter keeps well for up to 4 months in the refrigerator. Heat thoroughly before serving.)*

DESSERTS
AND BEVERAGES

INDIAN desserts are generally mellow milk- and fruit-based puddings that are welcome after a spicy meal. They can be made ahead and kept refrigerated for several days, making them ideal for entertaining.

Lassi—a frothy yogurt drink made with fruits, herbs, or flower essences—and fruit shakes, limeades, and lemonades are popular with Indian food because they counter the heat of the spicy food. Among alcoholic drinks served with Indian food, beer and ale are the most popular, and rightly so, since their malty effervescence complements the fragrant aromas and complex flavors of the food. Wine lovers need not despair, however. Any decent dry red, white, or rosé wine will go admirably as long as it is reasonably robust. Fine wines should be reserved for another occasion—their subtleties will be overpowered and lost when served with Indian food. You may of course serve non-alcoholic beer and wine or ice water as most Indians traditionally do.

QUICK SAFFRON PUDDING

Srikhand

This delicate pudding, made with yogurt and flavored with saffron, pistachios, and cardamom, comes from the state of Gujarat in western India. I find the process of draining yogurt time consuming, so I devised a shortcut. Combine yogurt with sour cream and cream cheese, and you can achieve the same flavor and richness. All this in less than a minute!

SERVES 4

1/4 teaspoon saffron threads, crushed

1 tablespoon hot milk or water

1 cup yogurt

1/3 cup sour cream

3 ounces plain cream cheese

2/3 cup confectioners' sugar

1/2 teaspoon ground cardamom

2 tablespoons chopped unsalted pistachios

1. Put the saffron threads in bowl. Add the hot milk and let soak for 15 minutes.

2. Add the yogurt, sour cream, cream cheese, and sugar and whip until thoroughly blended and light and fluffy. Stir in the cardamom and half the pistachios. Spoon the pudding into small dessert bowls or stemmed glasses. Sprinkle with the remaining pistachios. Refrigerate for at least 2 hours.

3. Serve chilled.

Variation

Fold in 2 cups cut-up fresh fruit with the pistachios.

Indian Rice Pudding
with Cardamom

Kheer

Rice pudding is one of the most popular desserts in India. There are many different versions but all have one thing in common: no eggs are used in the pudding. Instead, the milk is cooked down with the rice to a thick creamy consistency. This rice pudding, flavored with cardamom and coconut and garnished with raisins and almonds, is from Bengal, which is famous for its milk desserts.

SERVES 4

2 cups whole milk

3 cups light cream

1/4 cup basmati rice

1/4 cup sugar

1/2 teaspoon ground cardamom

2 tablespoons sweetened coconut flakes

2 tablespoons golden raisins,
   for garnish

2 tablespoons sliced almonds,
   for garnish

1. Combine the milk and light cream in a medium heavy-bottomed saucepan and bring to a boil over very low heat. Add the rice and simmer for 1 hour, or until the rice is cooked and the milk has reduced and thickened. Stir in the sugar, cardamom, and coconut. *(The pudding will keep, covered, for up to 5 days in the refrigerator.)*

2. Serve warm or chilled, garnished with raisins and almonds.

MANGO FOOL

Mangophul

Fool, a dessert of English origins, became the all-time favorite of Anglo-Indians. Here it is made with mango purée, but it can be done with any ripe fruit; it is particularly good with raspberries.

SERVES 4

1 large ripe mango

$^1/_2$ teaspoon almond extract

1 tablespoon lemon juice

2 tablespoons orange liqueur (optional)

1 cup light cream

$^1/_4$ cup sugar

2 tablespoons cornstarch dissolved in $^1/_4$ cup water

1 cup heavy cream, whipped

Mint sprigs, for garnish

1. Peel the mango and cut the flesh away from the pit. Purée the flesh in a food processor. Strain to remove any fibrous parts and put in a bowl. Stir in the almond extract, lemon juice, and liqueur. Set aside.

2. Heat the light cream and sugar in a small saucepan over medium heat. When small bubbles form around the edges of the cream, stir in the cornstarch mixture. Cook until the cream thickens and forms a custard, about 2 minutes. Strain the custard to remove any lumps and cool thoroughly.

3. Combine the mango purée and custard. Fold in the whipped cream, spoon into individual dessert glasses, and refrigerate for 2 hours. Serve garnished with mint.

Mango Ice Cream

Aam Kulfi

Indian ice cream is made without eggs. Milk and cream are cooked down, sweetened, and flavored. Fruit pulp—in this case mango—is stirred in before freezing. The result has a texture somewhere between ice cream and sorbet. Kulfi is traditionally made in special 3-inch-high conical aluminum or stainless steel molds with a lid. The frozen kulfi *is pried out with a knife; immersing the mold briefly in hot water aids this process.*

Serves 6

4 cups whole milk

1¹/4 cups heavy cream

¹/4 teaspoon grated nutmeg

5 tablespoons maple syrup or sugar

1 cup fresh mango purée or canned Indian Alphonso mango purée

1. Combine the milk and cream in a medium heavy-bottomed saucepan and bring to a boil over medium heat. Decrease the heat and simmer, stirring often, until reduced by half, to about 2¹/2 cups, about 20 minutes. Set aside to cool.

2. When cool, stir in the nutmeg, maple syrup, and mango purée. Pour the mixture into 6 *kulfi* molds or small ramekins, distributing it evenly. Cover with plastic wrap and freeze until set, about 6 hours.

3. To serve, remove the ice cream from the molds by running a sharp knife around the edges. If necessary, dip the mold in hot water to loosen it. Slip each *kulfi* onto a dessert plate, cut across into 3 or 4 slices, and serve.

SWEET MANGO LASSI

Aam Lassi

I guarantee that even if you think you don't like yogurt you will love this shake. Combined with mangoes and blended until frothy, lassi is always refreshing, not just at mealtime. The bubbly froth subsides when lassi stands awhile, so whip it again in the blender or with a whisk just before serving.

SERVES 4

3 cups yogurt

1 cup fresh mango purée or canned Indian Alphonso mango purée

$^1/_2$ cup sugar

$^1/_2$ cup water

1 tray ice cubes

Put all the ingredients in an electric blender or food processor and blend until the ice is crushed and the liquid is frothy. Serve immediately in tall glasses. *(The drink will keep, covered, for up to 3 days in the refrigerator. Whip again just before serving.)*

SAVORY YOGURT DRINK WITH MINT

Matha

A light drink made with diluted yogurt flavored with mint and cumin, this is a fabulous thirst quencher.

SERVES 4

3 cups plain yogurt

2 teaspoons lemon juice

1 cup ice water

1 tablespoon chopped mint or
  kari leaves

¹/₄ teaspoon ground toasted
  cumin seeds

1 tray ice cubes

Coarse salt

Put all the ingredients, including salt to taste, in an electric blender or food processor and blend until the ice is crushed and the liquid is frothy. Serve immediately in tall glasses. *(The drink will keep, covered, for up to 3 days in the refrigerator. Whip again just before serving.)*

GINGER LIMEADE

Shikanji

One of India's most popular beverages, limeade is classically made with an especially aromatic lime called the kagzee nimboo, *or paper-skinned lime. The American Key lime is the closest substitute. This drink is very delicious and refreshing, particularly when flavored with ginger.*

SERVES 4

¹/₄ cup lime juice

1¹/₂ teaspoons ginger juice (see Note)

³/₄ cup sugar

3 cups water

Ice cubes, for serving

Lime zest, for garnish

1. Combine the lime juice, ginger juice, sugar, and water in a tall pitcher and stir until the sugar is dissolved. Refrigerate for at least 2 hours.

2. To serve, fill tall glasses with ice cubes, pour the limeade over, and garnish with a twist of lime zest.

NOTE: To extract ginger juice, press peeled and chopped ginger through a garlic press. Two tablespoons ginger will yield 1¹/₂ teaspoons juice.

Variation

Stir 1 cup pineapple or pomegranate juice into the limeade.

SPICED TEA

Chai

The famous Indian spiced tea served in all Indian restaurants, chai is very refresh-ing to sip at any time of day, not just at the end of a spicy Indian meal. Generally, Indians drink their tea like the English, with sugar and milk. For Spiced Tea, it's best to use an Indian raw sugar, jaggery, that tastes like maple sugar rather than refined white sugar. I like this tea without the milk, but I added it as an option for those who want it. With or without the milk, this tea is truly magical.

SERVES 4

1 (3-inch) stick cinnamon

8 green cardamom pods, bruised

4 whole cloves

4 heaping teaspoons loose tea, or 4 tea bags, preferably orange pekoe or Darjeeling tea

2 to 3 tablespoons jaggery, crushed

4^1/2 cups boiling water

^{1}/3 cup scalded milk (optional)

1. Combine the cinnamon, cardamom, cloves, tea, and jaggery to taste in a warmed 8-cup teapot and pour the boiling water over. Cover the teapot with a potholder and let the tea and spices steep for 3 minutes.

2. To serve, strain into cups and pass the milk.

Variation

For a stronger tasting tea, combine all the ingredients, except the milk, in a saucepan and simmer for 2 minutes, until the water is infused with the dark color of the tea. Pass the milk, as above.

The Indian Pantry

Here is a checklist of spices, herbs, and other flavorings frequently called for in Indian cooking. Detailed descriptions follow.

SPICES, HERBS, AND SEASONINGS

Ajowan
Aniseeds
Asafetida
Bay leaves
Cardamom, green pods and seeds
Chiles, green
Cilantro
Cinnamon, sticks and ground
Cloves, whole and ground
Coriander seeds, whole and ground
Cumin seeds, whole and ground, toasted
Curry Powder (page 6)
Fennel seeds
Fenugreek seeds
Garam Masala (page 7)
Ginger, fresh and ground
Kari leaves, fresh or dried
Mint
Mustard, seeds and powder
Nigella seeds
Nutmeg
Panch Phoron (page 8)
Paprika
Peppercorns, black, white, green
Pepper, crushed red flakes
Pepper, ground red
Saffron, threads
Salt, coarse
Tamarind, paste or powder
Turmeric

COCONUT

Coconut flakes, sweetened and
  unsweetened
Coconut milk, fresh or canned
Coconut powder

JAGGERY

OILS, FLAVORINGS, AND OTHERS

Mustard oil
Spice-infused oils
Usli ghee

GRAINS AND LENTILS

Basmati rice
Chapati flour
Chickpea flour
Lentils, red
Yellow split peas

NUTS

Almonds
Cashews
Pistachios

RAISINS

Dark and Golden

LENTIL WAFERS

Glossary

An Indian kitchen is usually stocked with spices and dried herbs; lentils, peas, and beans; nuts and seeds; and oils and essences. Following are descriptions of the more common ingredients of Indian cooking.

Ajowan *(Ajwain)* Also known as carum, these tiny seeds resemble celery seeds. When slightly crushed, they give off an aroma similar to thyme. Ajowan is used with vegetables, fish, shellfish, breads, crackers, and especially beans and peas, since it counters flatulence. Thyme makes a good flavor substitute.

Aniseeds *(Saunf)* The tiny oval seeds of anise release the same aroma as fennel when crushed, though milder. Indian cooks prefer its subtle flavor to that of fennel. Anise and fennel are interchangeable in recipes.

Asafetida *(Heeng)* Asafetida is a combination of the resin from the rhizomes of certain plants that grow along the slopes of the Himalayan Mountains. The latex-like sap dries and turns into pungent smelling, brown, brittle lumps. In Indian cooking, asafetida is generally crushed and used in powdered form. The ground spice can be toasted, fried in oil, or boiled in liquid to release an aroma reminiscent of onions and garlic. Since vegetarians are prohibited from eating onions and garlic (seasonings associated with meat), asafetida makes a heavenly substitute. Heavy, starchy beans, peas, and vegetables often include asafetida as a flavoring because the spice is also a powerful digestive.

Since asafetida in its pure form has a tendency to cake, stabilizers such as rice flour or corn meal are mixed into the ground spice. Therefore, the commercially available powder has a creamy yellow color and a milder flavor. Good-quality ground asafetida is widely available at Indian and specialty grocers. The recipes in this book are tested with commercially available ground asafetida.

Basmati Rice *Basmati* means queen of fragrance in Hindi, and that is what this distinctive long-grain rice from India is. Naturally scented with buttery-almond flavor, the grains do not turn mushy or sticky when cooked. Basmati rice is widely available in health food stores and many supermarkets.

BAY *(TEJ PATTA)* Indian bay, the spicy and aromatic leaf of the cassia tree, is an essential spice in North Indian cooking. It is used in Moghul pilafs and curries and in the indispensible spice blend *Garam Masala*. Indian bay is available in Indian grocery stores. Commonly available bay leaf, which comes from the laurel tree, makes an acceptable substitute.

BLACK SALT *(KALA NAMAK)* Black salt is a unique smelling and tasting mineral deposit used as a spice in North Indian cooking. It is not technically a salt, so therefore cannot be used in place of white salt. Black salt comes in whole, lump form—which is black-colored, hence the name—or as a salmon-colored powder. Ground black salt is generally paired with ground roasted cumin seed to produce the distinct aroma characteristic of many North Indian *chats, raitas,* and chutneys. Ground black salt is available in Indian grocery stores.

CARDAMOM *(ELAICHI)* These are small, long green or white pods containing highly aromatic tiny black seeds. Cardamom is used either in the pod, as in pilafs and curries, or ground, in desserts and sauces. If used whole, the pods are discarded before serving. For ground cardamom, the pods are hulled, and the seeds separated from the membrane and ground to a powder.

CHAPATI FLOUR *(ATTA)* *Chapati* flour is finely ground whole wheat kernels with the germ and husk intact. It is rich in nutrients and flavor. Dough made with this flour is easy to roll. Stone-ground whole wheat flour can be substituted.

CHICKPEA FLOUR *(BESAN)* Also known as gram flour, chickpea flour is the ground meal of the chickpea legume. In Indian cooking, this flour is used in batters for fritters, dough for breads and wafers, and in sweets and candies. Chickpea flour is available widely in health food and specialty stores.

CILANTRO *(HARA DHANIA)* Cilantro, or fresh coriander, has a pungent aroma quite unlike the seeds of the plant. It is widely used in Indian cooking. Parsley can be substituted for visual appeal, but it lacks the distinctive taste of cilantro.

CINNAMON *(DALCHINI)* In Indian cooking, cinnamon is used in stick form to lend a subtle fragrance to pilaf and meat dishes and to add spice to tea infusions.

CLOVE *(LAUNG)* Fragrant and pungent, cloves are used both whole and ground in Indian cooking. Whole cloves are used when it is important not to tint the color of the dish, as in white rice pilaf and certain fish preparations. Remove the cloves before serving.

COCONUT *(NARIAL)* Coconut is extensively used in Indian cooking. Grated coconut is used to add texture and visual interest, coconut milk to give a sweet, rich flavor to a sauce. Excellent quality processed coconut is available in grated, milk, cream, and powder forms in Asian grocery stores. Light or heavy cream can be substituted for coconut milk to approximate the texture, with 2 tablespoons of coconut flakes for each cup of cream to approximate the flavor. Unsweetened coconut flakes can be substituted for freshly grated coconut. Freshly grated coconut and fresh coconut milk are simple to make.

> GRATED COCONUT *Buy a medium-size coconut that has no cracks and is heavy with liquid. Pierce the eyes of the coconut with a chisel, drain off the liquid, and discard. Place the coconut in a preheated 375° oven for 25 minutes. Remove the coconut and hit it with a hammer to crack it open and release the meat inside. Peel off the brown skin and cut the meat/flesh into 1-inch pieces. Working in batches, grind the coconut in a food processor. One medium coconut will yield about 2 cups grated coconut. Grated coconut keeps for 5 days in the refrigerator and 6 months in the freezer, stored in tightly sealed containers.*

> COCONUT MILK *Add 1¼ cups boiling water or milk to 1 cup grated coconut and let soak for 15 minutes. Working in batches, purée the mixture in a blender or food processor. Strain through a double layer of cheesecloth, squeezing the pulp to extract as much liquid as possible. One medium coconut will yield about 2½ cups coconut milk.*

CORIANDER SEEDS *(DHANIA SOOKHA)* Yellowish brown and about the size of peppercorns, coriander seeds have a mild and floral aroma. They are used in countless dishes in India, usually ground. Coriander is used in large quantities in both Curry Powder (page 6) and *Garam Masala* (page 7).

CUMIN SEEDS *(JEERA)* These tiny greenish brown seeds, resembling caraway in shape, are perhaps the most important spice in Indian cooking. Cumin is used both whole and ground and both raw and toasted. It is an important component of *Garam Masala* (page 7).

TOASTED CUMIN SEEDS Put ¹/₂ cup cumin seeds in a small dry frying pan over medium-high heat. Toast, stirring and shaking, until the seeds are several shades darker and give off their characteristic aroma, about 5 minutes. Transfer to a bowl and let cool. Using a spice mill, a coffee grinder reserved for grinding spices, or a mortar and pestle, grind to a fine powder. (Ground toasted cumin may be stored in an airtight container in a cool, dry place for 3 weeks.)

CURRY POWDER This spice blend from southern India works magic when creatively employed. In Indian cooking, it is used in soups, stews, sauces, and vegetable dishes. Curry Powder is widely available, but it is also very easy to make at home (page 6).

FENNEL *(SAUNF)* Fennel seeds, tiny and pale green in color, look like cumin or caraway seeds. Ground, they are used in sauces, sweets, and desserts. In Bengal, whole fennel seeds are cooked with vegetables and lentils. Fennel is an excellent digestive and a mouth refresher; it is frequently chewed by Indians like an after-dinner mint. Aniseed can be substituted.

FENUGREEK *(METHI)* These tiny, brown, bitter-tasting beans are an important spice, particularly in southern and eastern India. Known to counter flatulence, fenugreek is often added to starchy vegetables and legumes. Dill seeds can be substituted.

FLOWER ESSENCES *(RUH)* In Indian cooking, flower essences, such as rose (*gulab*) and Asian pine (*kewra*), are used to provide fragrance in much the same way as vanilla or almond extract. Flower essences are available in Indian and Middle Eastern grocery stores.

GARAM MASALA This highly aromatic blend of spices was created to season the Moghul dishes of northern India. It is sprinkled on or folded into a finished dish to give it a roasted flavor. *Garam Masala* is commercially available, but it can also be made easily at home (page 7).

GINGER, FRESH *(ADRAK)* Fresh ginger, the aromatic rhizome used extensively in Asian cooking, is important also in Indian cooking. It is used with vegetables and legumes, in pilafs and stews, in chutneys, and in herbal tea infusions. Since ginger is regarded as a digestive, it is added to dried beans, peas, and starchy vegetables. Fresh ginger is always peeled, using a peeler or paring knife, and then grated, crushed, chopped, or sliced. It will keep, loosely covered, for several weeks in the refrigerator. If fresh ginger is unavailable, ground ginger may be substituted (1 teaspoon ground ginger for 1 tablespoon fresh ginger).

GINGER, GROUND *(SONTH)* Ground ginger is made by powdering sun-dried slices of fresh ginger. It is used in Kashmiri meat dishes, kebabs, relishes, chutneys, sweets, desserts, and beverages. Although ground ginger can be substituted for fresh ginger, the two really aren't similar in taste. Ground ginger is sweet and woody while fresh ginger is spicy and herbal. Try to use the type specified in the recipe.

GREEN CHILES *(HARA MIRCH)* Green chiles add an herbal aroma as well as heat to a dish. If green chiles are unavailable, substitute 1/4 teaspoon ground red pepper for 1 green chile. For a milder taste, seed the chiles. For more of an herbal flavor, add a little chopped green bell pepper with the chiles. Chiles should be handled with care as they cause a burning sensation and irritation when touched. You may want to use rubber or surgical gloves to protect your hands. Take care not to rub your eyes. Be sure to wash your hands with soapy water after handling chiles.

JAGGERY *(GUDH)* Jaggery is unrefined cane or palm sugar. It is used in Indian cooking to lend a sweet taste and a maple-like flavor to the dish. Maple syrup or maple sugar can be substituted.

KARI LEAF *(KARI PATTA)* Kari leaf is an herb, not a spice. It should not be confused with Curry Powder, a blend of several spices (page 6). Kari leaves have a most captivating aroma, reminiscent of juniper berries and lime. They are used to flavor all types of savory preparations. Kari is better used fresh, though dried is acceptable. Fresh and dried kari leaves are available in Indian grocery stores.

LENTILS, RED *(MASAR DAL)* Red lentils, also called pink, are the most popular in Indian cooking because they cook quickly (in about 15 minutes) and are very easy to digest. They are cooked into thick purées, seasoned with spices, and served accompanied with rice or bread. Red lentils are widely available at health food stores.

LENTIL WAFERS *(PUPPADUM OR PAPAD)* These dried, paper-thin rounds are made from lentil or bean flour in a variety of flavors, ranging from plain to black pepper and garlic to green chile and cumin. When you fry them, they puff up (page 38). They are available at Indian grocery stores.

MINT *(PODINA)* Mint was the favorite herb of the Moghuls, who used it in their pilafs, kebabs, and special lamb dishes. Spearmint is preferred to peppermint. Use fresh mint rather than dried. If necessary, substitute 1 teaspoon dried mint for 1 tablespoon chopped fresh mint.

MUSTARD OIL *(SARSOON KA TEL)* Mustard seeds are pressed to yield a very aromatic, amber-colored oil that is widely used in the cooking of northern and eastern India. Because of its high smoking point, mustard oil is used for deep-frying. It is also used to flavor fish, shellfish, vegetables, and legumes. Mustard oil is available in Indian grocery and specialty stores.

MUSTARD SEEDS *(SARSOON)* These tiny round seeds, brown, black, red, or yellow, look like large poppyseeds. They are added to hot oil (always put the lid on since they spatter) and fried until they pop and release their fragrance. This mustard-infused oil is a prized seasoning in southern and eastern India. There is very little difference in flavor between various types of mustard seeds, so use whichever is available. Dry mustard and prepared mustard are also used in Indian cooking.

NIGELLA *(KALONJI)* These tiny, black teardrop-shaped seeds have a satiny sheen and a distinct celerylike taste. They have a natural affinity for fish, shellfish, and starchy vegetables. Because they are so beautiful, nigella seeds are always used whole. Also called black onion seeds.

NUTMEG *(JAIPHUL)* The Moghuls had a fondness for this spice and used it quite liberally in their pilafs and braised meats. Nutmeg is also used in sweets, desserts, and chutneys. Buy whole nutmeg and grate it as needed.

PANCH PHORON A classic from eastern India, this is a simple blend of five whole spices: cumin, fennel, mustard seeds, fenugreek, and nigella. It is used to make a spice-infused oil for cooking seafood, vegetables, and legumes. Preblended *Panch Phoron* is available in Indian grocery stores, but it can be made easily at home (page 8).

PANEER Soft, moist, crumbly, and imbued with lemon scent, the freshly made Indian cheese *paneer* is nourishing and flavorful. In Indian cooking, *paneer* is used crumbled and in cubes. It is available at Indian grocery stores. Farmers cheese and tofu can be substituted. Making *paneer* is very simple.

> PANEER *Bring 2 quarts milk to a boil. Add 3 1/2 tablespoons lemon juice and continue to cook, stirring, until the milk curdles and separates into curds and whey. Strain the curds through a colander lined with a double layer of cheesecloth. When cool enough to handle, gather together the corners of the cheesecloth and squeeze gently to extract as much liquid as possible. Remove the cheese from the cheesecloth, wrap tightly in plastic, and refrigerate. (The cheese will keep for 5 days in the refrigerator.) Makes 1 cup.*

PAPRIKA *(DEGHI MIRCH)* Paprika is dried and ground red pepper. Indian paprika, called *deghi mirch*, is different from the Hungarian, Spanish, or California paprika that we are more familiar with. Indian paprika, produced in Kashmir and Goa has a pungent aroma like cayenne, but with the spice's characteristic sweet flavor. Other paprika may be substituted. All paprika should be stored in the refrigerator.

PEPPER, BLACK *(GOL MIRCH)* Black pepper has been in India since ancient times. It is used extensively in all regions of India and in all kinds of dishes, including beverages and baking. While all peppercorns deliver the characteristic bite and scent, Tellicherry peppercorns are the most pungent and aromatic. Buy whole peppercorns and grind them as needed.

PEPPER, GROUND RED *(LAL MIRCH)* This is the red devil's powder that gives food a hot taste. By adding more or less of it, you can regulate the heat of a dish. Dried red chile pods ground to a powder, crushed red pepper, or fresh green chiles can be substituted.

PEPPER, WHITE *(SAFAID MIRCH)* White and black pepper are essentially the same except that white peppercorns are hulled to expose the grayish-white berries, unlike black peppercorns, which still have the dark skin attached. Because of their light color and delicate flavor, white peppercorns are preferred in cream sauces, cream soups, fruit salads, and certain fish and shellfish preparations of Anglo-Indian origin.

SAFFRON *(KESAR OR ZAFFRAN)* Saffron is the most expensive spice in the world. The Moghuls loved it and used it to flavor and color pilafs and meat casseroles. Saffron is also used in desserts, sweets, chutneys, and beverages. Buy only saffron threads, the pure form of the spice.

SALT *(NAWAK)* Salt is an essential component of Indian cooking, used not only to enhance but also to extract the flavor of spices and herbs. For general cooking, I prefer sea salt for its texture and purity.

SILVER LEAF *(VARK)* An edible paper-thin tissue of pure silver used as an adornment on foods for special occasions. If silver leaf is unavailable, omit it from the recipe.

SPICE-INFUSED OIL *(TADKA)* *Tadka* means exploded and that is exactly what happens when whole spices are added to very hot oil. In the *tadka* process, oil is heated in a small pan until very hot. Whole spices are then added and fried until they release their fragrance into the oil. This spice-infused oil is used as a base for dressing salads and for cooking vegetables, pilafs, chutneys, and other preparations. The three most popular *tadkas* of Indian cooking are cumin *tadka* from northern India, mustard *tadka* from southern India, and *Panch Phoron tadka* from eastern India.

TAMARIND *(IMLI)* Tamarind pulp, brownish-black in color with a distinctive sour taste, is used to flavor various soups, stews, sauces, chutneys, and relishes. Tamarind chutney and tamarind tea infusions are very popular in India. Tamarind is sold in 1-pound blocks, as a paste, and as powder. Pitted prunes combined with a little lemon juice or pomegranate molasses may be substituted.

TURMERIC *(HALDI)* This spice colors everything it touches yellow. It is one of the main ingredients of Curry Powder (page 6). Used in moderation, turmeric imparts a woody scent and light lemon color to pilafs, vegetables, and legumes.

USLI GHEE This melted and browned butter has a characteristic caramel-fudge aroma. It is used for pouring over *dal*, where a mere half teaspoon lends a mountain of flavor; for finishing fish or meat; and for cooking, mainly in pilafs, legumes, breads, desserts, sweets, and some soups. For centuries, the more common cooking medium has been, and still is, oils, such as sesame, peanut, mustard, and coconut oils. Clarified butter or vegetable oil can be substituted for *usli ghee.*

> USLI GHEE *Melt and simmer 1/2 pound (2 sticks) unsalted butter in a pan over low heat until it stops crackling and the residue at the bottom turns golden brown, about 25 minutes. When cool, strain off the clear liquid into a jar. Refrigerate or freeze. Makes 3/4 cup.*

YELLOW SPLIT PEAS *(CHANNA DAL)* Indian yellow split peas are the staple legume eaten by 700 million vegetarians in India. High in nutrients, they have many uses in Indian cooking, from soups and stews to dumplings, breads, and pancakes. The yellow split peas sold in American supermarkets are an acceptable substitute, but they are different botanically. Indian yellow split peas are meatier tasting and less gummy when cooked than their American counterpart.

YOGURT *(DAHI)* Yogurt is used in India to make sauces velvety and to mellow curries, and it is consumed as a salad, a dessert, and a beverage. To prevent the yogurt from separating when adding it to a warm sauce, lightly whip the yogurt first to stabilize it. Non-fat yogurt is fine in Indian cooking, but low-fat and whole milk yogurt will give creamier results. The choice is yours.

MAIL ORDER SERVICES

Adriana's Caravan
409 Vanderbilt Street
Brooklyn, NY 11218
(800) 316-0820
www.adrianas.com

Bazaar of India
1810 University Avenue
Berkeley, CA 94702
(510) 548-4110

Bombay Emporium
294 Craft Avenue
Pittsburgh, PA 15213
(412) 648-4965

Ethnic Grocer
555 West Madison
Atrium Level South
Chicago, IL 60661
www.ethnicgrocer.com

Foods of India
121 Lexington Avenue
New York, NY 10016
(212) 683-4419

Indian Grocery Store
2342 Douglas Road
Coral Gables, FL 33134
(305) 448-5869

Kalustyan's
123 Lexington Avenue
New York, NY 10016
(212) 685-3451
www.kalustyan.com

Kundan Foods
225 West 134th Street
Los Angeles, CA 90061
(310) 324-8877
www.kundanfoods.com

Patel Brothers
2610 West Devon Avenue
Chicago, IL 60659
(773) 262-7777

Patel Brothers
5815 Hillcroft
Houston, TX 77036
(713) 784-8332

Patel Brothers
1999 Hwy 80 West
Jackson, MS 39204
(601) 353-6611

Penzey's Spice House, Ltd.
P.O. Box 1448
Waukesha, WI 53187
(414) 574-0278
www.penzeys.com

The Souk
1916 Pike Place North
Seattle, WA 98101
(206) 441-1666

VIK Distributors, Inc.
726 Allston Way
Berkeley, CA 94710
(510) 644-4412

TABLE OF EQUIVALENTS

The ingredients in this book are measured in the standard American cup (8 ounces), tablespoon (16 tablespoons to a cup), and teaspoon (3 teaspoons to a tablespoon). For your convenience, weight equivalents for the most commonly used staples are provided in both ounces and grams and liquid equivalents in both ounces and milliliters.

WEIGHT EQUIVALENTS

	CHAPATI FLOUR		BASMATI RICE		LENTILS		JAGGERY		RAISINS		ALMONDS	
	oz	g	oz	g	oz	g	oz	g	oz	g	oz	g
1/4 CUP	1	30	1 1/2	45	1 1/2	45	1 1/2	45	1	30	1	30
1/3 CUP	1 1/2	45	2	60	2	60	2	60	2	60	2	60
1/2 CUP	2	60	2 1/2	75	3	90	3	90	3	90	2 1/2	75
1 CUP	4	120	5	150	6	180	6	180	6	180	5	150

LIQUID EQUIVALENTS (for milk, cream, yogurt, coconut milk, and stock, etc.)

	FLUID OUNCES (OZ)	METRIC MILLILITERS (ML)
1/8 CUP	1	30
1/4 CUP	2	60
1/3 CUP	2 1/2	80
1/2 CUP	4	125
1 CUP	8	250

INDEX